Motivating Literacy Learners in Today's World

Edited by Jo Fletcher, Faye Parkhill and Gail Gillon

NZCER PRESS

Wellington 2010

NZCER PRESS

New Zealand Council for Educational Research
PO Box 3237
Wellington
New Zealand

© Jo Fletcher, Faye Parkhill and Gail Gillon, 2010

ISBN 978-1-877398-65-0

All rights reserved

Designed by Cluster Creative

Printed by Thames Publications

Distributed by NZCER Distribution Services
PO Box 3237
Wellington
New Zealand
www.nzcer.org.nz

Contents

Introduction		5
Chapter 1	Motivating children to read through literature *Teresa Cremin*	11
Chapter 2	Motivating young writers *Noella Mackenzie*	23
Chapter 3	Writing in primary and middle schooling: Managing myths about student motivation *Judy M. Parr and Kathryn Glasswell*	33
Chapter 4	Supporting students who struggle with language *Elspeth McCartney and Sue Ellis*	43
Chapter 5	Phonological awareness: Motivating early literacy success *Gail Gillon and Brigid McNeill*	53
Chapter 6	Motivating children with dyslexia *John Everatt and Gavin Reid*	67
Chapter 7	Fostering story comprehension: Motivating struggling readers to engage in literature-based activities *Marleen F. Westerveld*	79
Chapter 8	Motivating Māori students in literacy learning: Listening to culture *Angus Hikairo Macfarlane*	89
Chapter 9	Motivating Pasifika students in literacy learning *Jo Fletcher, Faye Parkhill, Amosa Fa'afoi and Tufulasi Taleni*	99
Chapter 10	Asian student voices: Approaches in reading that motivate or provoke dissonance in their journey towards being successful readers of English *Faye Parkhill and Jo Fletcher*	111
Chapter 11	Playing with text *Janinka Greenwood*	121
Chapter 12	Multiliteracies and learning in a new age *Nicola Yelland*	133
Authors		147

Introduction

Being motivated to engage in speaking, listening, reading and writing is fundamental to sustaining and improving achievement in literacy. Children who experience success in literacy learning tasks that are appropriate, interesting and challenging are more likely to be motivated in their learning (Pressley, 2002). The teacher's role in supporting this motivation includes facilitating learning that is within a child's reach, providing scaffolding to support learning and monitoring students who are having difficulties. It also involves fostering the development of oral language, comprehension, vocabulary knowledge and writing skills; providing a range of interesting books; and, as much as possible, allowing children choice in their reading and writing (Guthrie & Humenick, 2004; Pressley, 2002).

Motivation to be a literacy learner involves inherent motivation in the form of a positive self-concept as a literacy learner, where there is a desire to speak, read and write, and an expression of enjoyment or interest in talking, listening, reading and writing. It includes the emotional engagement that children can have with literature. When children are engaged in literature they use their imagination, which allows them to move into other worlds. This extends social and personal development along with reading skills (Sainsbury & Schagen, 2004).

The first chapter, by Teresa Cremin, outlines how children can be motivated to read through literature. Cremin focuses on how teachers' knowledge and use of children's literature—along with a reading-for-pleasure pedagogy that encompasses rich reading aloud, time to read independently and talk about literature, and engaging social and physical reading environments—all combine to motivate reading. She highlights the concept of a reading teacher—a teacher who reads and a reader who teaches—and explores examples of how such teachers share their reading lives, creating reciprocal communities of motivated readers in the classroom.

The chapters by Noella Mackenzie, and Judy Parr and Kathryn Glasswell, explore motivational issues related to writing. Mackenzie focuses on the early years of writing, while Parr and Glasswell look at it from a middle school perspective. Mackenzie's chapter discusses how a child's drawing and talking can provide a powerful connection between home and school and offer both motivation and scaffolding for early writing. Learning to write becomes a natural extension of previous meaning-making experiences by building on what children already "know and can do" when they start school. Interactive writing provides the structure and opportunities for teaching children how to write.

Parr and Glasswell's chapter discusses the myths of managing motivation. They discuss how motivational issues take on greater importance as academic stakes increase across the years of schooling. Indeed, they become central in writing because it is through writing that students demonstrate their knowledge and understanding. This chapter explores notions of engagement in relation to learning to write by exploring some commonly held myths about writers and their engagement in writings tasks, and looking at the evidence for what really matters in relation to engagement in writing.

The chapter by Elspeth McCartney and Sue Ellis discusses the impact of oral language on success and motivation with reading and writing, and outlines how to support students who struggle with language. Some children in each class are likely to have speech, language and communication difficulties. Their oral comprehension and their ability to express themselves using language is compromised, which can cause social difficulties, but also difficulties in their school learning. Many struggle with literacy and school subjects, because similar skills underlie oral and written language. Keeping these children motivated and involved requires making adaptations to the classroom context to ensure that it is "communication friendly" and that children can signal when they have not understood, without penalty. In addition, direct teaching of relevant words, grammar and narrative structures can help them to cope.

The chapters by Gail Gillon and Brigid McNeill, and by John Everatt and Gavin Reid, discuss the issues surrounding motivation for students who struggle with decoding text. Gillon and McNeill discuss how all children need to be given the skills to become competent readers. Developing skills in phoneme awareness allows children to decode text, and the child is then not faltering at one of the "points of discouragement" (Byrne, 2007) that often occur on the pathway to reading mastery. Everatt and Reid help us to understand how students who exhibit the traits of dyslexia in their literacy learning can be supported and motivated to be successful readers. Following a brief introduction to dyslexia, they discuss an outline of the educational, behavioural and emotional problems associated with dyslexia. The chapter considers barriers of learnt helplessness and low self-esteem that can lead to poor motivation, and the difficulties involved in supporting children with dyslexia. Strategies for practice that might increase motivation, overcome barriers and improve learning are discussed.

Marleen Westerveld's chapter addresses the importance of oral language comprehension for successful reading acquisition and development, and the motivation to read. The chapter then investigates ways in which to engage struggling readers in literature-based activities that will foster the oral language skills required for reading comprehension.

The next three chapters examine how to support and motivate students from indigenous populations and other cultural groups. Angus Macfarlane's chapter focuses on how to motivate Māori students in literacy learning. He draws on a research project which offers ideas toward opening doorways for Māori learners. Huakina Mai is a shift away from the usual negative, self-defeating, deficit slants used by too many educators—toward promoting the actualisation of positive and well-meaning perspectives.

Jo Fletcher, Faye Parkhill, Amos Fa'afoi and Tufulasi Taleni outline what motivates Pasifika upper primary school children in the New Zealand classroom. These first-, second- or third-generation immigrant children encounter the challenges of learning to read and write in English, which is often a second language in their home and community. By understanding what these children perceive as supporting or providing barriers to literacy learning, teachers can actively promote culturally appropriate pedagogical approaches that support motivation and engagement in learning to read.

Faye Parkhill and Jo Fletcher's chapter focuses on Asian students situated in eurocentric classrooms. Asian students represent a diversity of cultural and linguistic identities—such as South Korean, Chinese, Malaysian and Taiwanese—and the authors discuss the risks in treating Asian students as a homogeneous group. The chapter identifies literacy practices that are conducive to learning for a diverse group of Asian students. These Asian students' beliefs about what motivates their literacy learning act as a frame of reference that can influence their thinking, feelings and actions towards learning.

In Janinka Greenwood's chapter on playing with text, she explores ways in which the creative and interactive processes of drama can be used to contextualise and animate text (of various kinds) and thereby motivate learners. In particular, she examines how a number of characteristics of drama processes—namely agency, the use of role and framing, deconstructive strategies and performance—can be actively manipulated to increase motivation in reading and to engage learners in negotiating the relationship between text and meaning. These concepts are illustrated by reference to several applied dramas designed to engage students in particular aspects of literacy.

Finally, Nicola Yelland's chapter discusses the notion of being multiliterate in the 21st century. She argues that we need to broaden our conceptualisation of being literate to incorporate fluency with digital technologies, which require a consideration of the various modalities of learning. The concept of multiliteracies enables us to think about contexts, modalities and ways of knowing in this new era. She interrogates what this entails for teachers and learners in today's schools and provides examples of learning scenarios from empirical research studies.

References

Byrne, B. (2007). Theories of learning to read. In M. J. Snowling & C. Hulme (Eds.), *The science of reading: A handbook* (pp. 104–119). Malden, MA: Blackwell.

Guthrie, J. T., & Humenick, N. M. (2004). Motivating students to read: Evidence for classroom practices that increase reading motivation and achievement. In P. McCardle & V. Chharbra (Eds.), *The voice of evidence in reading research* (pp. 329–354). Baltimore, MD: Paul H. Brookes.

Pressley, M. (2002). *Reading instruction that works: The case of balanced teaching* (2nd ed.). New York: Guilford Press.

Sainsbury, M., & Schagen, I. (2004). Attitudes to reading at ages nine and eleven. *Journal of Research in Reading, 27*(4), 373–386.

CHAPTER 1
Motivating children to read through literature

Teresa Cremin

Introduction

Children's literature is at the heart of the literacy curriculum. It plays a powerful role in the development of motivated and engaged readers and writers. It can arouse, inform and expand the horizons of the young, challenging their thinking and provoking multimodal responses. This chapter focuses on inspiring readers through engaging in literature, the importance of teachers' knowledge and use of literature, and the aesthetic satisfaction and connections to be gained. I also highlight the characteristics of a reading-for-pleasure pedagogy, which promotes diversity and desire, and examine the concept of a reading teacher—a teacher who reads and a reader who teaches (Commeyras, Bisplinghoff, & Olson, 2003), exploring how knowledgeable teachers create reciprocal communities of motivated readers.

Reading for pleasure

Extrinsically motivated readers read to satisfy the demands of others, reading for recognition, grades or competition, and to meet teachers' or parents' expectations (Wigfield & Guthrie, 1997). In contrast, readers who are intrinsically motivated are more likely to be reading for their own pleasure and satisfaction; such readers read more widely and frequently and enjoy their reading more (Cox & Guthrie, 2001). Reading for pleasure is associated with intrinsic motivation and is positively correlated with reading comprehension (Wang & Guthrie, 2004), although the relationship between intrinsic and extrinsic motivation is complex, and children may read for their own pleasure *and* be obliged to read for other purposes in school. What you read and the satisfaction you gain through reading can make a significant difference to your desire to read. However, as Woods (2001, p. 74) observes:

> it must be reading you do for yourself, at your own pace, in your own way, and that has a bearing on your own background, interests, values, beliefs and aspirations.

Although the teaching profession needs to pay more attention to children's diverse textual preferences in the 21st century, it also needs to acknowledge and foster a love of literature, of fictional worlds and of the power of narrative and poetry, which helps to develop readers who not only can read, but who choose to read.

In finding personal resonances in literature, readers make meanings, consider other world views and form new insights into their own. Young readers deserve to encounter texts that have particular salience for them so that they can come to value the experience and be caught in a web of fiction that motivates them to renew such an imaginatively revitalising experience. As one 10-year-old commented, "reading makes me feel everything more deeply, it's like being in a hot tub in my imagination" (Cremin, 2007 p. 175). Other children and adults also assert that the affective dimension is a key motivator (Dungworth, Grimshaw, McKnight, & Morris, 2004; Spufford, 2002). Yet without teachers who know which books to recommend to which readers, young people may never connect to the power of literature or find themselves in printed fiction.

Teachers' knowledge of children's literature

Internationally, research indicates that successful literacy teachers are knowledgeable about children's literature, prioritise the importance of meaning and teach through whole texts (Block, Oakar, & Hurt, 2002; Medwell, Wray, Poulson, & Fox, 1998). Yet such knowledge is frequently taken for granted in lists of required teacher competencies. A recent United Kingdom Literacy Association (UKLA) survey revealed that although primary phase professionals are adult readers of fiction and recognise the deep imaginative value that literature can offer, their knowledge and use of children's literature is limited (Cremin, Bearne, Mottram, & Goodwin, 2008b). The 1,200 teachers in this survey relied on a canon of authors and their own childhood favourites, and had particularly inadequate repertoires of poetry and picture fiction: 22 percent and 24 percent of the sample, respectively, did not or could not name a single writer in these categories (Cremin, Bearne, Mottram, & Goodwin, 2008a). Arguably, such teachers, 85 percent of whom reported relying on their own repertoires to select books for school, were merely using fiction and poetry as a resource for instructional purposes. They were also heavily over-dependent on "celebrity" authors such as Roald Dahl and J. K. Rowling at the expense of a wider range, and were not in a position to motivate readers through their own knowledge of children's literature.

In response to this issue, the UKLA project Teachers as Readers: Building Communities of Readers (known as TaRs) was designed to improve children's pleasure in reading through widening teachers' knowledge and pedagogic use of children's literature, and broadening their personal knowledge and understanding of being a reader. This year-long project involved 43 teachers from five local authorities in extensive professional development that encompassed both national and local development days. The focus was on reading children's literature more widely and setting personal goals and targets for this; sharing their new knowledge with others; exploring classroom activities to support reading for pleasure; reflecting on their own independent reading practices and considering the implications for pedagogy and practice. A mixed methods design was employed so that the team could explore numerical trends and qualitative evidence from the whole project, as well as observations and interviews in the 10 case study schools. The teachers each studied three disaffected readers whose attitudes towards reading improved considerably across the year, as did their perceptions of their abilities and self-confidence as readers. These findings were evidenced in the children's questionnaires and interviews, the teachers' records and interviews, and researcher observations. The data also revealed that, for a range of reasons, including more control and more time, the number of children choosing to read at home and at school increased significantly over the course of the year. The focus on children's more positive reading mind sets and the increase in voluntary reading also appeared to influence their attainment, which, as graded by the national assessment system, increased significantly (Cremin, Mottram, Collins, Powell, & Safford, 2009).

This research revealed that when teachers read children's literature widely for their own pleasure and construct a potent reading-for-pleasure pedagogy, positioning themselves as reading teachers who share their reading lives with young learners, then new reader relationships developed that significantly influenced the children's attainment and achievement (Cremin et al., 2009).

I now turn to the key insights from this research to illuminate the characteristics of the reading-for-pleasure pedagogy and the nature of the reading teachers' practices that had an impact on the children's desire to read.

A reading-for-pleasure pedagogy

Children who are not motivated to read fail to benefit from being taught reading (Guthrie & Wigfield, 2000). So although instructional work is essential, teachers also need to plan to enhance engagement and reading for pleasure. The social, emotional and cultural dimensions of being a reader need to be recognised and fostered so that communities of readers can be built that acknowledge the diverse cultural capital and home literacies of the young. Enticing invitations need to be offered to hear, read, inhabit, explore and respond to potent texts. Such invitations have the potential to increase learners' confidence and interest in reading. The TaRs project, undertaken in 27 schools across England, indicated that an effective reading-for-pleasure pedagogy, which fosters reader agency and motivation, includes extensive reading aloud, regular time for young people to talk about their reading, as well as space for independent free-choice reading in a supportive environment (Cremin et al., 2009).

Reading literature aloud

If the day-to-day reading experiences model the pleasures and positive purposes of reading, this can help motivate children to read voluntarily. Dedicated time for teachers reading aloud to children is therefore vital. This daily encounter with the language of written text provides a rich sense of the shapes of stories and poems (Purcell-Gates, 1988) and access to sophisticated themes and literary language beyond the children's independent reading capacities. In the TaRs project, teachers tempted children to read more and helped build their familiarity with authors, poets and illustrators by creating classroom "texts in common", which the teachers read to the class (Cremin, 2010). For example, as one teacher noted, "A girl brought in *Breadwinner* by Deborah Ellis set in Afghanistan for me to read, saying she thought I would like it—I did and read it to the class." (Cremin et al., 2009, p. 25).

Also, when teachers voice their own responses to literature during such whole-class teacher read-aloud sessions, this can help prompt children's aesthetic responses and trigger questions that foster interest and enrich comprehension. Teachers need to choose richly reverberative texts that bear re-reading and prompt children's active engagement through related activities (e.g., dance, drama, music, art, discussion and writing) appropriate for the age group of the listeners, which help them to explore the meanings, identify with characters and situations and make life-to-text and text-to-life connections. Over time, in a community of readers the TaRs teachers found that pupils were helped by reading aloud to other classes and sharing their knowledge of the literature that inspired them.

Time for independent reading

Regular time for independent reading is important because it offers space for imaginative engagement and sharing, and can help sustain the habit, developing persistence. Daily recreational reading can significantly improve children's reading abilities (Taylor, Frye, & Maruyama, 1990), although the degree of pleasure involved will relate closely to the reading material. Some research suggests that lower income children consistently have less access to reading materials (Nueman & Celano, 2001), so teachers need to ensure the choice of books provided by the school is constantly updated, as well as enriched by everyday reading materials such as comics, magazines, newspapers, periodicals and catalogues.

A culturally relevant range of texts is necessary not only to increase the possibility of making connections, but also to ensure that reading is not removed from its sociocultural context. Privileging particular types of texts or marginalising popular cultural or media texts should be avoided, because schools need to build on pupils' own reading interests as well as introduce them to potent literary texts. In the TaRs project, free-choice reading-time sessions became more frequent and lasted longer, offering children access to a wider range of texts. Children were not expected to read alone in silence, although some chose to do so; others socialised and shared their reading with each other and with their teachers (Cremin et al., 2009).

Time to talk about literature—reader to reader

Book talk is crucial for developing readers' understanding of the multilayered meanings of texts, and is a powerful motivator because it involves honouring children's own responses, questions, connections and thoughts (Chambers, 1993). A pedagogy that focuses on reading for pleasure should offer dedicated time for discussion and collaboration, enabling pupils to make open interpretations, share their preferences and widen their desire. Routinising textual encounters and focusing on comprehension and criticism can reduce the likelihood that learners will become affectively involved; instead, teachers will want to exploit possibilities and gaps in texts (Iser, 1978) that offer space for personal engagement. As one 11-year-old boy in the TaRs project commented:

> Open book time is the best thing we've ever done in school … ever. You get to talk to each other about what everyone is reading … anything at all … you can share bits or read bits to each other. It makes you want to read something that other people are talking to you about. (Cremin et al., 2009, p. 27).

Talking about texts with interested peers in informal contexts, where teacher assessment is not foregrounded, can be highly motivating and can help sustain and support newly involved readers.

A supportive reading environment

Although the school reading environment is important, teachers' awareness of the "funds of knowledge" (Moll, Amanti, Neff, & Gonzalez, 1992) children bring to school, as well as home–school–community partnerships, may need to be strengthened to help motivate young readers. In the TaRs project, teachers prioritised building classroom communities, although a few brokered new relationships beyond the school based on children's everyday reading practices. In school, new spaces—both physical spaces and time spaces—were created for teachers and children to talk about their engagement in particular texts. The physical spaces involved the creation of reading tents, "big blue sofas", reading corners and reading cafés, which were more social and encouraged new forms of informal interaction around reading. The new time-space related to parts of the day when relationships were less structured, book talk was more free and collaborative and child-initiated "insider text talk" was triggered (Cremin et al., 2009).

These two types of reading spaces shared one identifiable and underlying component: affect. They nurtured children's personal encounters with literature and other texts, and helped build new reader relationships. The spontaneous child-initiated text talk in classrooms and on the playground revealed an accumulated history of shared reading experiences and common textual knowledge. This "legacy of past satisfactions" (Britton, 1993), satisfactions that were shared, began to deepen their desire to read more, especially when they were supported by a reading teacher.

Reading Teachers: Teachers who read and readers who teach

Research studies in the US highlight a connection between teachers who are keen readers and children who are keen readers (Bisplinghoff, 2002; Commeyras et al., 2003). In the UK the TaRs research confirms this connection, demonstrating that when teachers share their reading lives and love of literature explicitly, this strongly influences pupils' knowledge about and pleasure in literature, fostering their development as motivated readers. In summarising the US research, Dreher (2003) notes that teachers who are engaged readers are motivated and socially interactive about what they read, as well as strategic and knowledgeable as readers, and that this helps to develop students who are in turn engaged readers. However, some of the 43 TaRs teachers expressed reservations about sharing something of themselves and their reading habits and processes in class. In a highly visible accountability culture, several perceived it to be too personal a position to adopt, while others were not convinced that the time spent sharing their reading lives would pay dividends.

Only around 40 percent of the teachers fully explored the transformative potential of this personal/professional identity shift. However, those who took up the position of fellow reader in the classroom community, and explored the relationship between their own reading practices and preferences and those of the children, found there was immense value in this new, more personal stance in relation to motivating readers (Cremin et al., 2009). Through documenting their reading histories and practices, these teachers became more aware of their journeys as readers and began to share their insights, making their practices and strategy thinking more public. In addition, they became more aware of contexts conducive to reading, both social and environmental, and sought to recreate such comfortable and informal contexts in school, as noted above.

Their increased awareness of themselves as readers clustered around four areas: texts, habits, strategies and emotional response. Although seemingly a simple shift, the consequences of this repositioning were significant: these professionals created more opportunities to develop children's metacognitive awareness of themselves as readers and created more overtly reciprocal reading communities in class. They took part not merely as assessors or instructors, but as readers: readers with a passion and a perspective. As one observed, "I realise it's about being a role model—I think about myself as a reader and I talk to the children—well, as a reader—about reading" (Cremin et al., 2009, p. 15). They profiled reader agency and many explored Daniel Pennac's (1992) list of "Rights of a Reader" in his book *Reads Like a Novel*, recognising that adult and child readers should both be allowed, for example, to choose to leave a book unfinished or to reread a favourite text. Not surprisingly, perhaps, the children in the reading teachers' classes made the most progress in terms of attainment and achievement as readers.

Conclusion

In order to motivate young readers, teachers need to balance literacy instruction, which tends to focus on decoding and comprehension, with a reading-for-pleasure pedagogy, which focuses more on engagement and response. As the Organisation for Economic Co-operation and Development (2002) argues, and the TaRs project shows, the will to read influences the skill. In this UK research—when teachers read widely to young learners and shared their own enthusiasm and love of literature, offering them time to read and talk about texts of their own choosing—the majority of the previously disaffected case study readers became highly motivated, and their attainment levels were raised. The personal affective stance of the reading teachers, which foregrounded meaning, pleasure and purpose, appeared to fuel the children's desire and foster their delight, perhaps laying the foundations of a life-long habit and ongoing satisfaction in reading.

Implications for practice

Consider your own practice. Do you include all the key elements of a reading-for-pleasure pedagogy? Do you share your own reading life with children, positioning yourself as a reading teacher? What aspects of your practice and position deserve further development?

References

Bisplinghoff, B. S. (2002). Under the wings of writers: A teacher who reads to find her way. *Reading Teacher*, 56(3), 242–252.

Block, C., Oakar, M., & Hurt, N. (2002). The expertise of literacy teachers: A continuum from preschool to Grade 5. *Reading Research Quarterly*, 37(2), 178–206.

Britton, J. (1993). *Literature in its place*, Portsmouth, NH: Boynton/Cook/Heinemann.

Chambers, A. (1993). *Tell me: Children, reading and talk*. Stroud: Thimble Press.

Commeyras, M., Bisplinghoff, B. S., & Olson, J. (2003). *Teachers as readers: Perspectives on the importance of reading in teachers' classrooms and lives*. Newark, NJ: International Reading Association.

Cox, K. E., & Guthrie, J. T. (2001). Motivational and cognitive contributions to students' amount of reading. *Contemporary Educational Psychology*, 26(1), 116–131.

Cremin, T. (2007). Revisiting reading for pleasure: Diversity, delight and desire. In K. Goouch & A. Lambirth (Eds.), *Understanding phonics and the teaching of reading* (pp. 166–190). Berkshire: McGraw Hill.

Cremin, T. (2010). Poetry teachers: Teachers who read and readers who teach poetry. In M. Styles & M. Rosen (2010). *Poetry and childhood*. London: Trentham.

Cremin, T., Bearne, E., Mottram, M., & Goodwin, P. (2008a). Exploring teachers' knowledge of children's literature. *Cambridge Journal of Education, 38*(4), 449–464.

Cremin, T., Bearne, E., Mottram, M., & Goodwin, P. (2008b). Primary teachers as readers. *English in Education, 42*(1), 1–16.

Cremin, T., Mottram, M., Collins, F., Powell, S., & Safford, K. (2009). Teachers as readers: Building communities of readers. *Literacy, 43*(1), 11–9.

Cremin, T., Mottram, M., Collins, F., Powell, S., & Safford, K. (2009). *Teachers as readers: Building communities of readers*. Leicester: Primary National Strategy and UKLA.

Dreher, M. (2003). Motivating teachers to read. *The Reading Teacher, 56*(4), 338–340.

Dungworth, N., Grimshaw, S., McKnight, C., & Morris, A. (2004). Reading for pleasure?: A summary of the findings from a survey of the reading habits of year 5 pupils. *New Review of Children's Literature and Librarianship, 10*, 169–188.

Guthrie, J. T., & Wigfield, A. (2000). Engagement and motivation in reading. In M. L. Kamil, P. B. Mosenthal, & P. D. Pearson (Eds.), *Handbook of Reading Research: Volume 3* (pp. 403–422). New York: Erlbaum.

Iser, W. (1978). *The act of reading*. Baltimore, MD: Johns Hopkins University Press.

Medwell, J., Wray, D., Poulson, L., & Fox, R. (1998). *Effective teachers of literacy: A report of a research project commissioned by the teacher training agency*. Exeter: University of Exeter.

Moll, L., Amanti, C., Neff, D., & Gonzalez, N. (1992). Funds of knowledge for teaching: Using a qualitative approach to connect homes and classrooms. *Theory into Practice, 31*, 132–141.

Nueman, S. B., & Celano, D. (2001). Access to print in low-income and middle-income communities: An ecological study of four neighborhoods. *Reading Research Quarterly, 36*(10), 8–26.

Organisation for Economic Co-operation and Development. (2002). *Reading for change: Performance and engagement across countries: Results from PISA 2002*. New York: Author.

Pennac, D. (1994). *Reads like a novel*. London: Quartet Books.

Purcell-Gates, V. (1988). Lexical and syntactic knowledge of written narrative held by well-read-to kindergartners and second graders. *Research in the Teaching of English, 22*(2), 128–160.

Spufford, F. (2002). *The child that books built*. London: Faber.

Taylor, B. M., Frye, B. J., & Maruyama, G. M. (1990). Time spent reading and reading growth. *American Educational Research Journal, 27*(2), 351–362.

Wang, J. H. Y., & Guthrie, J. T. (2004). Modelling the effects of intrinsic motivation, extrinsic motivation, amount of reading, and past reading achievement on text comprehension between US and Chinese students. *Reading Research Quarterly, 39*, 162–186.

Wigfield, A., & Guthrie, J. T. (1997). Relations of children's motivation for reading to the amount and breadth of their reading. *Journal of Educational Psychology, 89*, 420–432.

Woods, P. (2001). Creative literacy. In A. Craft, B. Jeffrey, & M. Liebling (Eds.), *Creativity in education* (pp. 62–79). London: Continuum.

CHAPTER 2
Motivating young writers

Noella Mackenzie

Introduction

Learning to write involves the "hand, eye, and both sides of the brain" (Bromley, 2007, p. 244) and is one of the most complex of the many new challenges children face when they start school. Furthermore, children's success with early writing has a direct impact on their ability to engage with most other literacies, including reading. Children come to school with a range of meaning-making systems that have been working well for them in their prior-to-school contexts. These systems might include play, oral language, music and drawing. Many children also have experience with electronic games, computers and multimodal texts. Some start school with print experience, although few have mastered this abstract two-dimensional form of "meaning making" which is so highly valued and promoted once children enter school (Mackenzie, 2008).

Children have much to learn about the writing process before writing can become an efficient system of communication in the way that oral language, play and drawing are when they start school. They can, however, be motivated to want to add writing to their meaning-making repertoire if they can see how it builds on what they already know and can do and has purpose and relevance to their lives.

This requires providing them with opportunities to learn the new skills they need, when they need them, from a more knowledgeable other whom they know and trust. The teaching of writing is as complex for teachers as the learning of writing is for children. One effective way to make the connections between the known and the new is to start the writing programme with a focus on drawing and talking.

Drawing and writing

Drawing is a "constructive process of thinking in action, rather than a developing ability to make visual reference to objects in the world" (Cox, 2005, p. 123). Young children are not taught to draw, but innately and compulsively draw to explore and "play with" their world (Norris, Mokhtari, & Carla, 1998). Although drawing is recognised as a legitimate means of communicating and an important aspect of literacy in its own right (Shagoury, 2009), in this chapter the focus is on the relationship between drawing and writing. Most children entering school are intrinsically motivated to draw and will continue to draw if their drawing work is valued by the people they know and trust, particularly their teacher. Drawing and writing involve many of the same psychomotor skills, depend on similar cognitive abilities, are both expressive arts, are both developmental and are both purposeful (Jalongo, 2007). If writing is introduced as a parallel means of meaning making rather than a replacement for drawing and talking, children will learn to make choices about the most appropriate and effective ways of communicating for specific purposes. The texts that young children can create when they combine drawing and writing are generally more complex and meaningful than when they use just one or other system. Sadly, in many classrooms drawing is treated as a precursor to writing, which quickly disappears in the first year of school or is something to be done when the real work (writing) is completed—if time permits.

Research over the past 30 years reports a strong relationship between emergent writing and drawing (Baghban, 2007; Dyson, 1988, 1990; Grinnell & Burris, 1983; Norris et al., 1998; Ring, 2006; Shagoury, 2009). Despite this, the findings from a recent study (2007–9) conducted by the author into how early writing is taught in contemporary kindergarten classrooms in New South Wales (Australia) suggest that some teachers might not encourage drawing as a meaning-making process, nor as a support for early writing. This trend, which has also been reported in the UK (Coates & Coates, 2006), may be a response to the "accountability movement" (Genishi & Dyson, 2009, p. 59), a consequence of a "narrow understanding of literacy as reading and writing words" (Ring, 2006, p. 195), or a view of drawing as a time filler or "an activity to encourage realistic representations of objects, people, places or events" (Einarsdottir, Dockett, & Perry, 2009, p. 5).

Although children begin to sort out the differences between drawing and writing at a very young age, the relationship between the two systems remains critical (Grinnell & Burris, 1983). Some reports suggest that drawing pictures before, during or after writing helps children compose and interpret meaning from print (see, for example, Baghban, 2007; Kress, 1997; Shagoury, 2009). Drawings may also provide an external representation of ideas and reduce the cognitive demands of writing on working memory (Grinnell & Burris, 1983). Early writing attempts are restricted by students' limited knowledge of the skills and rules involved (spelling, concepts about print, etc.) , but when they are combined with drawings the messages have a richness that is impossible for the neophyte writer to achieve with writing only (see Figure 1).

Talking and writing

Although most children enter school capable of conducting complex conversations with adults and peers, they still have much to learn about language and how it is used at school. Drawings and their accompanying narratives provide perfect opportunities to link prior-to-school and school experiences, existing knowledge with new knowledge and current language usage with the new meta-language of school literacy. These conversations may also confirm that children have something worthwhile to share with others, therefore motivating them to draw and write. The more classroom language is a co-construction, the more teachers and learners come to share understanding about goals, performance of tasks, participation and the meaning of guidance in the classroom, the more effective the interactions between them will be (McNaughton, 2002, p. 122). Co-construction opportunities such as those afforded by interactive writing provide many opportunities for rich exploration, extension and expansion of language.

Figure 1 Independent writing sample from a child in the first year of school

Talking, drawing and writing

A study conducted by the author in 2009 involved kindergarten teachers actively encouraging children (during the first six months of school) to draw and talk about their drawings during "daily, independent writing time". Independent writing was introduced as a natural extension of children's drawings (and talk) rather than a replacement or superior system of expression. Writing conventions were introduced through interactive writing lessons. Teachers modelled drawing in much the same way as they would model writing and demonstrated how to "edit" by returning to previous drawings to make changes or add details. Children were encouraged to take pride in their drawings, which were shared and displayed. In some classrooms, artists' circles provided a more formal opportunity for children to share and discuss their drawings.

Teachers discovered the importance of listening to children as they were drawing and talking. The oral narratives that accompanied children's drawings became valued as teachers realised that the end products only told part of the story. Children were highly motivated by this approach. In the sample in Figure 1, Sam[1] wrote, "I am going to Ulladulla. The crabs are running away from the swordfish", when he had been at school for less than four months. This sample illustrates how drawing and writing have been effectively combined to create quite a complex text. The opportunity to talk about his text allowed Sam to utilise another strength and form of expression—oral language. A discussion between the teacher, the child and some other children added further details as he talked about "the fisherman, his boat, his fishing line and his catch". Sam was encouraged to use his strengths in drawing and talking to support his developing skills as a writer. Interactive writing lessons were used to teach the conventions of writing that Sam needed to get him started as a writer.

Interactive writing

Interactive writing is a collaborative teaching and learning strategy that supports the development of both reading and writing processes. It is particularly powerful in the first two years of school. Interactive writing can be used to teach children the skills, strategies and conventions they need for conventional writing, but it also provides the opportunity for idea development and vocabulary expansion. These daily lessons involve the teacher and a group of children jointly composing and constructing a short written message (usually just one sentence per day in early kindergarten). The strategy is designed to utilise what children already know and can do (collectively), to teach them new skills, and to provide reasons for writing.

Interactive writing lessons begin with a discussion of potential topics that are of relevance to the class or group (e.g., a shared experience or a topic being explored in another part of the curriculum). On Monday this is a new topic. The message is written on an interactive whiteboard or large chart paper and built up over the week. From Tuesday to Friday the lessons start with the group reading what was written on the previous day/s. This process provides many opportunities for rereading and discussion of how to move forward. At strategic points in the

---

1 A pseudonym.

writing process individual children are invited by the teacher to take the shared pen and write specific letters, letter clusters, words or punctuation (things the chosen child can succeed with). This is highly motivating because all children have the chance to contribute over time. In some classrooms children are given particular responsibility for a specific high-frequency word for a period of time (e.g., John is responsible for writing "to" each time it is needed this week). An alphabet chart and "word wall" are used as writing resources.

Across the week the group learns how to write new high-frequency words (two or three per week at the start of the year and more as the year progresses) and explores writing conventions, letter–sound relationships (phonemic awareness and phonics), spelling patterns, letter formation, vocabulary, sentence structure, use of space, editing processes, etc., based on the teacher's choice as to what offers "high instructional value" (Brotherton & Williams, 2002). The teaching takes place at the point of need and is of relevance to all students because they have shared authorship—and therefore ownership—of the co-constructed text. The teacher and children frequently reread what they have written to check their work. At the end of each lesson the teacher summarises the learning for the day and encourages children to apply this learning to their own writing. The text is displayed so that children can return to it whenever they wish. Once an important word is added to the word wall, children are encouraged to check with each other and/or the word wall when they are writing these words.

In the example below (from a kindergarten classroom early in the school year), the letter patterns and sight words that were singled out by the teacher for instructional purposes have been underlined. The words "and", "can" and "are" were identified as important words for all children to learn and were added to the word wall as they were introduced ("to", "be" and "in" were already on the word wall, along with a number of other high-frequency words that had been introduced on previous occasions). Children practised how to write the words that were added to the word wall using individual whiteboards. On Tuesday they practised writing "and" as well as learning that "some" was like "come" but with a different first letter. They had been introduced to "come" in a previous lesson and had been playing with onset and rime patterns in other lessons. Discussion of the difference between real and pretend bears led to a debate about which books they had been sharing that were factual and which were fictional.

Writing topic: What we know about bears
Gri<u>zz</u>ly bears grow to b<u>e</u> ver<u>y</u> big. (Composed and jointly constructed on Monday)
<u>Some</u> bears sl<u>ee</u>p in caves <u>and</u> <u>eat</u> fish. (Tuesday)
Panda bears <u>are</u> black and white. (Wednesday)
Bears <u>can</u> run ver<u>y</u> fast. (Thursday)
<u>Rea</u>l bears are smart and to<u>y</u> bears are very cu<u>ddly</u> and good to take to bed. (Friday)

Throughout the week the teacher helped the children see that a number of their words had different ways of writing the long *ee* sound: Grizzl<u>y</u>, ver<u>y</u>, b<u>e</u>, sl<u>ee</u>p, <u>ea</u>t, r<u>ea</u>l, cuddl<u>y</u>. (Note: for a more comprehensive explanation of interactive writing, refer to Brotherton and Williams, 2002.)

Independent drawing and writing time

Independent drawing and writing time should follow interactive writing, either immediately or later in the day. At this time teachers encourage children to draw pictures of something that is of interest to them (from a shared or personal experience), share the drawing with other children at their table and then add some writing to their drawing. Children are encouraged to talk and help one another as they work. Teachers listen, observe, encourage and provide teaching assistance where appropriate. Some teachers focus on one group each day. They take every opportunity to remind children what they have been learning in interactive writing that could help them with their own writing. If children ask the teacher for assistance with words that are on the word wall, the teacher encourages them to locate the word on the word wall with the help of a friend. For other words, children are encouraged to apply their developing letter–sound relationship knowledge and have a go at hearing the sounds in the new word and recording them.

Implications for practice

Young school starters are natural learners, with unlimited potential and motivation for learning, who will apply themselves to whatever they believe will help them with their ongoing exploration of their world. Most young children crave success in the new school environment, and if they see an advantage in being able to write, they will apply the same focused attention to learning how to write that they applied to learning to be oral language users. However, having children who want to learn how to write is only part of the challenge. Teachers must take the new learning (in this case writing) to the child so that it dovetails with what they already know and can do. The forms of expression that children are already successfully using when they start school (talking, drawing and playing) provide the link to what is relevant to them. Teachers should encourage children to continue to explore and develop the skills of drawing and talking while teaching them how to write as a new and useful form of expression. This kind of teaching will never come in a one-size-fits-all package because it requires teachers to be knowledgeable, flexible and responsive to the ever-changing needs of their students.

The approach to teaching writing to young children that has been described in this chapter leads to children who:
- are highly motivated to draw, talk and write
- are flexible in their approach to writing
- are not dependent on teacher-provided topics or story stems
- want to draw and write in free time
- work collaboratively, helping each other to solve problems
- see writing as a natural extension of drawing and talking.

Two very experienced kindergarten teachers who participated in the Mackenzie study (2010) made the following comments when asked to identify the most successful, elements of their writing programme in 2009:

> The most successful element was the drawings ... in other years children sometimes said, 'I don't know how to write', but because we started with the drawings they always had something to write about, they always had something to say ... (Teacher 1)

That we started with drawings . . . it's ridiculous how simple this concept is and yet I had never done it before . . . this year there were never any blank pages . . . the drawings helped them start and continued to act as a motivator and reminder of what they were writing about . . . they could go back and forth from drawing to writing. (Teacher 2)

Drawing and talking provide a ready-made scaffold and motivation for the new learning that children need to take on as they engage in the writing process.

References

Baghban, M. (2007). Scribbles, labels, and stories: The role of drawing in the development of writing. *Young Children, 62*(1), 20–26.

Bromley, K. (2007). Best practices in teaching writing. In L. B. Gambrell, L. M. Morrow, & M. Pressley (Eds.), *Best practices in literacy instruction* (pp. 243–263). New York: Guilford Press.

Brotherton, S., & Williams, C. (2002). Interactive writing instruction in a first grade literacy program. *Journal of Reading Education, 27*(3), 8–19.

Coates, E., & Coates, A. (2006). Young children talking and drawing. *International Journal of Early Years Education, 14*(3), 221–241.

Cox, S. (2005). Intention and meaning in young children's drawings. *International Journal of Art and Design Education, 24*(2), 115–125.

Dyson, A. H. (1988). *Drawing, talking, and writing: Rethinking writing development*. Berkeley, CA, and Pittsburgh, PA: Center for the Study of Writing.

Dyson, A. H. (1990). Symbol makers, symbol weavers: How children link play, pictures, and print. *Young Children, 45*(2), 50–57.

Einarsdottir, J., Dockett, S., & Perry, B. (2009). Making meaning: Children's perspectives expressed through drawings. *Early Child Development and Care, 179*(2), 217–232.

Genishi, C., & Dyson, A. H. (2009). *Children, language and literacy: Diverse learners in diverse times*. New York and London: Teachers College Press.

Grinnell, P. C., & Burris, N. A. (1983). Drawing and writing: The emerging graphic communication process. *Topics in Learning & Learning Disabilities, 3*, 21–32.

Jalongo, M. R. (2007). *Early childhood language arts* (4th ed.). Boston: Pearson Education.

Kress, G. (1997). *Before writing: Rethinking the paths to literacy*. London: Routledge.

Mackenzie, N. M. (2010). *From drawing to writing: How does making drawing a priority in the writing program affect the teaching and learning of writing in the first six months of school?* Manuscript submitted for publication.

Mackenzie, N. M. (2008). Becoming a writer: Can we predict how children will engage with the writing process at school entry? *Journal of Reading, Writing & Literacy, 3*(1), 1–18.

McNaughton, S. (2002). *Meeting of minds*. Wellington: Learning Media.

Norris, E., Mokhtari, K., & Carla, R. (1998). Children's use of drawing as a pre-writing strategy. *Journal of Research Reading, 21*(1), 69–74.

Ring, K. (2006). Supporting young children drawing: Developing a role. *International Journal of Education Through Art, 2*(3), 195–209.

Shagoury, R. E. (2009). *Raising writers: Understanding and nurturing young children's writing development*. Boston: Pearson Education.

CHAPTER 3

Writing in primary and middle schooling: Managing myths about student motivation

Judy M. Parr and Kathryn Glasswell

Introduction

Research on emergent and early writers suggests that the desire to write, and solving the task of performing as a writer (McNaughton, 1995), is critical in the early stages of learning to write (Clay 1987; Czeirenwski, 1992). As time goes on, writing becomes seen by some students as having more to do with work than with communication, and self-expression, enthusiasm and word counts dwindle (Glasswell, 1999). As schooling progresses, students apply their writing skills in many knowledge domains. Academic tasks become more complex, and writing is increasingly the mode through which students demonstrate their knowledge and understanding of what they learn. They also learn to use writing to explore and expand their own thinking. Early in their school careers writers need to be nurtured in ways that develop certain dispositions and beliefs about writing and its importance. They need help to develop a writer's identity that includes self-perceptions of competence and tenacity (Atwell, 1987; Calkins, 1994).

In any discussion about writers who struggle with motivation, we think of William, a Year 5 writer whom we have written about previously (Glasswell,

Parr, & McNaughton, 2003). William's teacher described him as "hard work" as a writer, and for him writing was indeed "work". He struggled to write even a few words. When we asked him why kids did writing at school, he said to show others (teachers and parents) what they could do—a performance view. He did not talk in a way that would indicate a commitment to writing as a form of self-expression or of communication with others. Nor did he talk about writing as rewarding and enjoyable. His beliefs about writing were reflected in his behavior during writing lessons: he was inattentive and wrote very little. Conference interactions during which William worked individually with his teacher to discuss his writing were short, often interrupted, and offered little scope to his teacher. His written texts were brief. William disliked writing, and by Year 5 he was already accomplished at avoiding it.

The research tells us that writers like William are not uncommon in primary and middle-school classrooms, and their behaviours and dispositions have been widely described (e.g., Atwell, 1987; Graves, 2003). Teaching writing effectively involves understanding the complexity of motivational issues and the impact they have on writing success. However, first we need to understand why some students find writing difficult, and then we need to know what to do to make engaging in writing tasks easier and more enjoyable to help achieve a positive outcome. To tackle these issues, in this chapter we question two apparently straightforward ideas that teachers we work with commonly hold about motivation and writing:
- Interested writers are always better writers.
- Believing in yourself is your key to success as a writer.

We describe these ideas as myths, because each one, while not an entirely accurate account, has some truth in it. Our aim here is to unpack these myths in research terms so that we might better understand what really matters when motivating writers.

Myth 1: Interested writers are better writers

There are several ways this myth about motivation contributes to classroom practices that may not actually be helpful in getting the desired results of more and better-quality writing. Many professional books for teachers send the message that learner writers need to be interested in the topic, task or activity they are writing about to produce better quality writing. Teachers are encouraged to assist students to find topics that are personally motivating (Calkins, 1994; Graves, 2003). To do this, teachers either leave topic choice to students, believing that self-generated or self-chosen topics are superior to imposed ones, or they spend considerable time and effort devising interesting topics and activities in an effort to engage students.

What the research shows

It transpires that the relationship between interest and better writing is not straightforward. When we think of interest, we picture someone paying close attention, concentrating and experiencing positive feelings in relation to some object, event or idea. This may be in response to a particular situation that has arisen (situational interest), or it may be a more long-term, individual interest. Both of these can contribute to what, in relation to writing, is called topic interest. Motivation to write can certainly be increased if students are enabled to write on topics of interest to them. But this does not necessarily result in better writing or an increased amount of writing. It is content knowledge that plays a major role in the quality of writing produced. It is not enough for writers to be interested in what they write about; they also need to know something about the topic (Hidi & McLaren, 1991).

Although research shows that content knowledge interacts with topic interest, there is yet another related factor that affects writing quality. The old saying "Never mind the quality, feel the width" encompasses it. Basically, we argue that although quality is not necessarily related to the quantity of text written, the amount of text a writer can generate can have far-reaching consequences. Our own study showed that motivated high-progress writers tended to write over twice as much as low-progress writers, and that this gap widens with age (Glasswell, 1999). The associated instructional and social benefits of this difference in word production gave "good" writers the edge in terms of the potential to engage more productively and successfully than students who wrote less. Peter Elbow (1973) was not just making a play on words when he talked of needing to write in order to learn to write. Practising the craft of writing means having opportunities to acquire fluency.

Sometimes, efforts to engage students by teachers who believe that interested writers make better writers can have unintended consequences. This happens when teachers try to motivate writers by providing stimuli in the form of lessons, artefacts and extended discussion. Timperley and Parr (2009) suggest that some teachers treat motivation to write as a separate component of writing tasks instead of something integral to contexts where writing is a meaningful communicative activity. Their study, which involved examining writing lesson blocks, showed that about 80 percent of the time that teachers gave to writing was used in prewriting activities, such as those designed to exchange experiences, and only 20 percent was spent recording ideas on paper and sharing the resulting pieces. The authors argue that such practices can have undesirable consequences, because time for thinking ideas through and for writing is reduced, as is the practice factor associated with writing fluency. Thus, activities designed to promote motivation to write clearly need to be balanced against opportunities to write extended and developed texts that express ideas and opinions and communicate information, and with time for specific and targeted writing instruction.

Related to interest is the notion of *ownership*. Where students perceive ownership, they report higher intrinsic motivation. Social constructivist theory sees motivation emerging from the intrinsic value of literate activities, activities that are part of the cultural and social fabric. Writing is a meaningful activity that provides its own motivation because it is a social activity involving expressing and communicating thoughts and ideas to others and receiving responses from them. A way to give students ownership over their writing is to ensure *authentic* writing experiences (Bruning & Horn, 2000): those that involve students in writing for enjoyment and communicative purposes, as opposed to learning skills for some unclear future task (Hiebert, 1994).

Implications for teaching

Motivation to write is affected by the opportunities to write on meaningful topics, and students having background knowledge and a reason or purpose for writing. Students need opportunities to write about topics relevant to their background knowledge and experiences (Benton, Sharp, Corkill, Downey, & Khramtsova, 1995;

Turner, 1995). Learning through meaningful, hands-on activities has a positive effect on motivation. As opposed to simply reading a text or listening to something described by the teacher and then writing, allowing students to take ownership of their learning by actually participating in and experiencing the content in a meaningful context, increases motivation. Also, real-world interactions help students to use the background knowledge they might have with respect to a given learning goal. This is especially important because students in today's classrooms bring with them a wealth of different experiences. Providing them with opportunities to incorporate their knowledge and experiences, and to create background knowledge through hands-on interaction with new material, creates curiosity, intrinsic motivation and personal goals for knowledge seeking (Perencevich, 2004).

Myth 2: Believing in yourself is key to success as a writer

Teachers we meet often place great emphasis on each writer's self-confidence. Beliefs writers hold about their abilities influence what they do with the skills and knowledge they have (Bandura, 1986). Beliefs affect outcomes for students by "influencing the choices they make, the effort they expend, the persistence and perseverance they exert when obstacles arise, and the thought patterns and emotional reactions they experience" (Pajeres, 2003, p. 140). They are like a filter through which experiences are interpreted.

What the research shows

Although belief in oneself as a writer is important, the research tells us that it is a specific kind of belief that is necessary if writers are to succeed. The beliefs students hold about themselves as learners play a major role in academic success or failure. Self-efficacy for writing has been clearly linked to writing achievement (Pajares & Johnson, 1996; Shell, Murphy, & Bruning, 1989), and this relationship exists from primary school to tertiary level (Pajares & Valiante, 2006).

Self-efficacy is related to motivation. It is different from self-confidence in that it is not just a general belief, such as "I am a good writer". Rather, it relates much more closely to specific sets of skills that a writer possesses. These might relate to specific aspects of knowledge about language, skills and strategies. It is useful to think of self-efficacy as confidence coupled with strategic problem solving, with a good measure of tenacity or stickability thrown in. A positive sense of self-efficacy in approaching a range of writing tasks, and for specific dimensions of writing, is an essential part of a writer's resource set. Further, supporting the development of self-efficacy will provide a key motivational driver for writing.

It is important, therefore, to understand how we form the perceptions that make up our sense of self-efficacy. Although they are essentially personal constructions, they derive from the environment (Bandura, 1986). One way we build them is from our interpretations of how well we have done in the past. If you are accustomed to receiving a good grade or comment, but then get a relatively poor grade or comment, your self-efficacy might decline and decisions you make about future effort are likely to be affected. We also inform our beliefs by observing others and making comparisons.

An important source that informs students' beliefs about themselves comes from the classroom environment, including feedback from teachers. Research suggests that classrooms with performance-oriented learning goals (such as the goal to gain an "achieved well") may foster maladaptive learning behaviours. This emphasis on grading is more common as students advance through the school system and is associated with students feeling less competent (Anderman & Midgley, 1997). When teachers highlight performance differences between students, some writers are more likely to self-handicap with behaviours such as procrastination, lack of effort and excuses. These are not surprising responses in situations where students feel inadequate about their efforts. With this goes a lack of motivation to participate or to succeed, and such students are less likely to succeed (Urdan, 2004). Another result of performance-oriented classrooms is that students do not ask for help, because asking for help when they need it might draw attention to their inability to perform a task (Ryan, Pintrich, & Midgley, 2001).

Implications for teaching

An important aspect that contributes to students feeling self-efficacious is a sense of control. Because writing is such a demanding activity and students have to make many decisions, writing requires self-regulation. Self-regulation involves the various self-initiated thoughts, feelings and actions a writer uses to achieve goals. Helping students to become more self-regulated learners through the use of strategies improves performance and attitude, and also builds self-efficacy (Graham & Harris, 2000) through knowing they have the tools to do the job.

In writing, to help improve self-efficacy we can teach strategies and self-regulation. A strategy provides structure that helps a writer to organise and sequence behaviour. Self-regulation skills are needed to help students recognise when to use a strategy successfully. In work by Steve Graham and his colleagues, task-specific strategies for writing, such as planning and revising, were combined with procedures for regulating the use of these strategies in the writing process (Harris, Graham, Mason, & Saddler, 2002). This work also included learning to control behaviours like negative self-talk or impulsivity, and to use self-regulatory processes such as self-assessment and goal-setting. These researchers describe an instructional sequence—or meta-script, as they call it—which includes developing and activating background knowledge; discussing the purpose and benefit of the strategy; modelling the strategy; and memorising (often using acronyms) the procedural steps for using the strategy and the self-regulation procedures. This meta-script is supported through temporary and adjusted assistance, which is reduced over time and combined with extensive opportunities to practise independently.

This type of instruction can work in a normal classroom. A colleague of ours showed that the use of a meta-script has great benefits in the classroom (Year 9) and can have a positive effect on writing (Hawthorne, 2008). Students' beliefs that they can complete tasks on their own makes them feel they have more freedom of choice as writers. The belief that they are in control of their actions and engagement makes them feel more competent and that they have more self-efficacy. This, in turn, fuels motivation.

Final thoughts

Labelling as "unmotivated" those students who do not engage in writing tends to place the emphasis and responsibility on the individual, with correspondingly little or no emphasis on the environments in which students learn. What we have discussed here are the complex interrelations among learners' agency (interest and ownership) and autonomy (including self-regulation, self-evaluation and control), environmental features such as meaningful contexts for writing and the teacher's emphasis on grades, and social factors, including support and feedback. All of these variables have the potential to affect the way students approach academic tasks—within which writing is central—and their motivation to engage in them.

References

Anderman, E. M., & Midgley, C. (1997). Changes in achievement goal orientations, perceived academic competence, and grades across the transition to middle schools. *Contemporary Educational Psychology, 22*, 269–298.

Atwell, N. (1987). *In the middle: Writing, reading, and learning with adolescents.* Portsmouth, NH: Boynton/Cook.

Bandura, A. (1986). *Social foundations of thought and action: A social cognitive theory.* Upper Saddle River, NJ: Prentice Hall.

Benton, S. L., Sharp, J. M., Corkill, A. J., Downey, R. G., & Khramtsova, I. (1995). Knowledge, interest, and narrative writing. *Journal of Educational Psychology, 87*(1), 66–79.

Bruning, R., & Horn, C. (2000). Developing motivation to write. *Educational Psychologist, 35*(1), 25–37.

Calkins, L. (1994). *The art of teaching writing.* Portsmouth, NH: Heinemann.

Clay, M. M. (1987). *Writing begins at home: Preparing children for writing before they go to school.* Auckland: Heinemann.

Czerniewska, P. (1992). *Learning about writing.* Oxford: Blackwell.

Elbow, P. (1973). *Writing without teachers.* New York: Oxford University Press.

Glasswell, K. (1999). *The patterning of difference: Teachers and children constructing development in writing.* Unpublished doctoral thesis, The University of Auckland, Auckland.

Glasswell, K., Parr J. M., & McNaughton, S. (2003). Working with William: Teaching, learning, and the joint construction of a struggling writer. *Reading Teacher, 56*(5), 494–500.

Graham, S., & Harris, K. R. (2000). The role of self-regulation and transcription skills in writing and writing development. *Educational Psychologist, 35*(1), 3–12.

Graves, D. (2003). *Writing: Teachers and children at work* (2nd ed.). Portsmouth, NH: Heinemann.

Harris, K., Graham, S., Mason, L., & Saddler, B. (2002). Developing self-regulated writers. *Theory into Practice, 41*, 110–115.

Hawthorne, S. (2008). *Engaging reluctant writers: The nature of reluctance to write and the effect of a self-regulation strategy training programme on the engagement and writing performance of reluctant writers in secondary school English*. Unpublished doctoral thesis, The University of Auckland, Auckland.

Hidi, S., & McLaren, J. (1991). Motivational factors and writing: The role of topic interestingness. *European Journal of Psychology of Education, 6*, 187–197.

Hiebert, E. H. (1994). Becoming literate through authentic tasks: Evidence and adaptations. In R. B. Ruddell, M. R. Ruddell, & H. Singer (Eds.), *Theoretical models and processes of reading* (pp. 391–413). Newark, DE: International Reading Association.

McNaughton, S. (1995). *Patterns of emergent literacy: Processes of development and transition*. Auckland: Oxford University Press.

Pajares, F. (2003). Self-efficacy beliefs, motivation, and achievement in writing: A review of the literature. *Reading and Writing Quarterly, 19*, 138–158.

Pajares, F., & Johnson, M. J. (1996). Self-efficacy beliefs and the writing performance of entering high school students. *Psychology in the Schools, 33*(2), 163–175.

Pajares, F., & Valiante, G. (2006). Self-efficacy beliefs and motivation in writing development. In C. A. MacArthur, S. Graham, & J. Fitzgerald (Eds.), *Handbook of writing research* (pp. 158–170). New York: Guilford Press.

Perencevich, K. C. (2004). How the CORI framework looks in the classroom. In J. T. Guthrie, A. Wigfield, & K. C. Perencevich (Eds.), *Motivating reading comprehension: Concept oriented reading instruction* (pp. 25–53). Mahwah, NJ and London: Lawrence Erlbaum.

Ryan, A. M., Pintrich, P. R., & Midgley, C. (2001). Avoiding seeking help in the classroom: Who and why? *Educational Psychology Review, 13*(2), 93–114.

Shell, D. F., Murphy, C. C., & Bruning, R. H. (1989). Self-efficacy and outcome expectancy mechanisms in reading and writing achievement. *Journal of Educational Psychology, 81*, 91–100.

Timperley, H. S., & Parr, J. M. (2009). What is this lesson about? Instructional processes and student understandings in the writing classroom. *Curriculum Journal, 20*(1), 43–60.

Turner, J. C. (1995). The influence of classroom contexts on young children's motivation for literacy. *Reading Research Quarterly, 30*(3), 410–441.

Urdan, T. (2004). Predictors of academic self-handicapping and achievement: Examining achievement goals, classroom goal structures, and culture. *Journal of Educational Psychology, 96*(2), 251–264.

CHAPTER 4
Supporting students who struggle with language

Elspeth McCartney and Sue Ellis

Introduction

This chapter considers children who have speech, language and communication difficulties. These can result from insufficient quality or quantity of language experience, or they may arise developmentally, despite appropriate language input from families and carers. They may or may not be associated with impairments such as hearing loss, learning disabilities, cerebral palsy or autistic spectrum disorders.

Whether children's difficulties are specific to language learning or are more general, it is important that these children become motivated, engaged learners. Motivation is central, but not in itself enough to guarantee high engagement. Engaged readers are intrinsically (rather than extrinsically) motivated to read, and have the required resources and strategies to do so. Meta-analyses show that strategy teaching, curricular coherence, choice, social collaboration and purpose all have an impact on reading engagement (Guthrie & Wigfield, 2000). In turn, motivation and engagement have an impact on attainment through mechanisms such as practice effects and perseverance. Continued engagement is therefore particularly important for children with speech, language and communication needs. Where language is part of the problem, children are at significant risk of literacy difficulties persisting into adult life (Law, Rush, Schoon, & Parsons, 2009).

Children with difficulties form a worryingly large group in mainstream education, and meeting their needs will be the responsibility of most teachers at some time in their careers. Lee (2008, p. 7) suggests that "on average, every primary school classroom in the UK will have two or three children who have some form of speech language and communication needs". Children whose language impairment is fairly specific often leave school with lowered school attainments (Conti-Ramsden, Durkin, Simkin, & Knox, 2009). Many report lowered self-esteem until the end of compulsory schooling, related to their academic difficulties. Lowered self-esteem appears to be an outcome of literacy difficulties rather than a cause, and post-school contexts when literacy difficulties become less intrusive coincide with higher self-esteem (Lindsay, Dockrell, & Palikara, 2009).

Unlike typically developing children, or those for whom English is a new language, children who struggle with language often find it difficult to learn new words. They must hear them many more times than other children if they are to absorb their meanings and use them. When they meet a new word, whether written or spoken, they may have difficulty breaking it down into its morphological or phonemic segments. They may also have relatively few related words stored in their semantic system, which makes understanding definitions and explanations difficult (see, for example, Nash & Donaldson, 2005). They may also find it difficult to remember long sentences with complex clause structures, as found in many reading materials, or to remember information across paragraphs (reviewed by Gajria, Jitendra, Sood, & Sacks, 2007).

As a result, their difficulties may include decoding written text and understanding text meanings. Writing can be even more challenging, requiring adherence to spelling, sentence construction and genre conventions. Children with speech, language and communication difficulties are coping with ongoing and taxing difficulties that require teachers to have knowledge of specific supporting strategies, in addition to those needed to motivate and engage all children.

General motivating factors

Guthrie and Humenick (2004) outline the aspects of the curriculum that create engagement, and these are summarised below:

- Teaching pedagogies that actively promote *curricular coherence* and *strategy teaching* means that children are taught strategies that will "travel" from one lesson and context to another, and are encouraged to see how these can be applied to their learning across the curriculum. This may require quiet, but important, shifts in current pedagogies rather than brand new approaches. For example, when teaching children strategies, teachers often ask them to identify, at the end of a particular lesson, what they have learnt. However, if teachers were to ask children when they might next use (and practise) these strategies and knowledge, it could increase curricular coherence.
- *Purposeful tasks* that foster intrinsic, rather than extrinsic, motivation and create mastery-oriented rather than performance-oriented conditions are also important. In mastery conditions, pupils become interested in ideas, learning processes, the level of challenge and the strategies used; in performance-oriented tasks they focus on attainment outcomes and on gaining a competitive advantage over others.
- Opportunities for children to *exercise choice* and to engage *with interesting, relevant and stimulating tasks and texts* also increase their engagement and motivation to read.
- Finally, opportunities for and expectations of *social collaboration* in learning tasks and contexts create engagement. Collaborative tasks encourage intrinsic motivation and promote self-efficacy and persistence. Children are more likely to "have a go" at complex tasks, and persist when they encounter difficulties, if there is a collaborative, social element to their learning.

A growing body of research has identified counter-productive socio-environmental processes that demotivate pupils and allow negative learning behaviours to thrive. Stanovich (1986) coined the term "Matthew effects" to describe how small differences in learning to read during a child's first year of school can have lasting and compounding effects. Stanovich's study showed that children who made a slower start in the most visible aspect of reading, decoding words, could quickly become caught up in a downward learning spiral: they found reading difficult and experienced fewer incidental opportunities to practise, which meant they fell behind others who were grabbing every possible opportunity to read. As children began to realise they were less competent, they began to actively avoid reading, which ensured they got even less practice—further widening the gap between the highest and lowest attainers.

Moss (2007) draws on ethnographic evidence to explain why some boys who find themselves in classroom contexts that place a high emphasis on reading proficiency choose to read nonfiction books. They might not actually prefer nonfiction, but are aware that fiction texts signal their competence as a reader by the amount of text on the page, the length of the book and the size of print. Nonfiction texts may not do this so overtly, making them particularly appealing to status-conscious boys who are not high achievers in reading. Also, the pictorial nature of many nonfiction texts and the reader's pre-existing knowledge of the topic often allows them to be discussed without necessarily being read.

Moss's research is a caution against adopting simplistic explanations about literacy behaviours and translating them unquestioningly into policy and practice. Her work would suggest that flooding schools with nonfiction texts on the grounds that "boys like to read them" might not produce the positive results on reading attainment that policy makers and schools desire. Being aware of such fundamental issues, how they are embedded in the social fabric of the classroom and how they affect motivation are essential knowledge for teachers.

Motivating and engaging children with speech, language and communication difficulties

In addition to motivating factors that apply to all children, others are specific to engaging children with speech, language and communication difficulties. These are discussed under four headings: maintaining a "communication-friendly" classroom; penalty-free signals of comprehension difficulties and obtaining clarification; direct language teaching; and sources of help and advice for teachers.

Maintaining a communication-friendly classroom

"Communication-friendly" classroom practices are not new to teachers: they are basic teaching skills. However, they are particularly important for increasing the motivation and engagement of children who struggle with language. Learning and Teaching Scotland (2000) details 19 principles, which have been compressed by McCartney, Ellis, and Boyle (2009) into six themes covering classroom organisation, management and teacher interactions:

- *enhancing the physical environment,* by creating good visual and listening conditions
- *planning communication partners and opportunities for talk,* by ensuring that children are in supportive and responsive peer groups, with only one child talking at a time, and with encouragement to express thoughts and feelings
- *planning topics* of interest to children, with clear advance warnings of a change of topic
- *offering visual support and demonstration,* by showing what is expected using pictorial support, experiential learning, games and role playing
- *verbal* aspects of teacher interaction, including using short and simple sentence constructions, simplifying and repeating instructions and giving instructions one at a time
- *nonverbal* aspects of teacher interaction, which involves providing natural but clear talk that is not too loud, too fast or too slow and exaggerated; making good eye contact; talking only when not facing the board; and limiting teacher movement around the classroom.

McCartney et al. (2009) note that these features of a communication-friendly classroom can be difficult to achieve. Teachers often have little control over background noise or lighting levels, topic choice or a topic's interest to individuals, and limited opportunities for group work. Verbal and nonverbal aspects of teacher communication are highly routinised and difficult to change. Nevertheless, in that study teachers did report adaptations to their interaction to support children with language difficulties. Teachers simplified their instructions, checked for child attention and understanding and became aware of their rate and clarity of speech.

Comprehension difficulties and clarification

Crucially, in a communication-friendly classroom it is acceptable to ask for and receive clarification because one does not understand. There are often penalties for asking teachers to rephrase or repeat: it risks signalling that one has not understood when others have, and there is the danger of being thought inattentive, or worse. There is also a social challenge in asking for clarification. It could suggest that the teacher did not communicate clearly and so might seem cheeky or challenging. For such reasons, children's clarification requests to teachers are less frequent than those of teachers to children, although it is children who have the comprehension problems.

In Scotland, some of these ingrained difficulties are being challenged by the Scottish Government's Assessment is for Learning programme (Learning and Teaching Scotland, 2010). Teachers use techniques to get instant feedback on their teaching. For example, a show of thumbs indicates how knowledgeable, confident or competent pupils feel about a particular activity or teaching point: thumbs straight up indicate high confidence; thumbs parallel to the floor indicate the learner is less clear about what is required, or what has been taught; and thumbs pointing down indicate that a learner is thoroughly confused and would like the task or teaching point to be completely re-explained.

Other ways of encouraging clarification requests and active listening have been developed (Dollaghan & Kaston, 1986; Johnson, 2000). These stress that despite listening carefully and paying attention in class, from time to time people will not understand each other. This is no one's fault: sometimes acoustic conditions are bad, or a speaker uses words unfamiliar to the listener and/or sentences that are too complicated, or a listener just misses a bit. The important thing is to recognise and remedy the misunderstanding. If the listener identifies the problem, they should feel safe in asking the speaker to revise without being thought rude. If the speaker feels the listener may have misunderstood, they check to see if a clarification would be helpful and offer a repetition or rephrasing. No one ridicules anyone, no eyes are rolled or sighs are sighed. It is safe to admit to the problem.

Again, such ideas are not new to teachers and can benefit all children, but they do require specific teaching to children with language difficulties. A classroom culture that allows clarification and improved understanding is a positive, motivating environment. Only when unrecognised do problems remain unrepaired.

Direct language teaching

Children with speech, language and communication needs may also benefit from direct teaching of linguistic elements. Teaching new vocabulary at the point it is needed in curriculum work is helpful. Teaching links to other words (e.g., synonyms, antonyms and categories) can help fix a word in the semantic system and reinforce its meaning, as can definitions and illustrations. Linking the word with its written form at the same time, and discussing its phonological and morphological patterns, can help to "glue" a new word in memory. This is often done with curricular content words. However, Boyle, McCartney, Forbes, and O'Hare (2007) developed an efficacious intervention for children with expressive language impairments in which vocabulary learning was heavily oriented to common English words, including content and relational terms (e.g., *either/or* and *unless*), sequential words (e.g., *first*, *next* and *last*), and words with specific meanings in mathematical contexts. Such words are important for understanding oral and written instructions and when dealing with curriculum areas such as science. Teaching them at the point of need—and giving regular reminders—can demystify the curriculum and help motivation.

Other areas may also require direct teaching, including the grammatical structures encountered in written texts, which differ considerably from those in spoken language; tracking meaning throughout a text; narrative and story grammars; and the rules for good oral or written stories. The important thing is to create a culture that allows learning and success, and thereby enhances motivation.

Sources of help and advice for teachers

There are resources available to school staff to support them in developing motivating classes. We have produced resources for teachers, which have been developed and validated in research studies (McCartney, Ellis, Boyle, Turnbull, & Kerr, in press). Our *Language Support Model for Teachers* was developed with teachers and speech and language therapists to support children with specific language impairments in mainstream primary schools. This is adaptable to other contexts and offers practical guidance on how to: create a communication-friendly classroom; encourage comprehension monitoring; and teach (as necessary) vocabulary, grammar and oral narrative. It is free to download from http://www.strath.ac.uk/eps/courses/slt/lms.html.

There is also advice for teachers working with children with particular difficulties. In the UK the National Deaf Children's Society produces "deaf-friendly" materials, available for schools (free international registration from http://www.ndcs.org.uk/). The British Association of Stammering has information for secondary schools supporting children who stammer at http://www.stammeringineducation.net. The Scottish Government's Autism Toolbox at http://www.scotland.gov.uk/Publications/2009/07/06111319/0 gives suggestions for organising classrooms and learning for children on the autistic spectrum. These are just examples: many organisations concerned with the welfare of particular groups of children offer similar resources and advice to motivate and engage children who struggle with language.

Final words

No learning—and especially no language learning—can be divorced from the social and emotional context in which it takes place. In a celebrated editorial, Richard Allington (2005) responded to a US National Reading Panel report (National Institute of Child Health and Human Development, 2000), which identified five pillars of scientific reading instruction (phonological awareness, phonics, fluency, vocabulary and comprehension). Allington accepted these as critical, but proposed five additional pillars detailing the purposes and contexts of learning to read (interesting texts and choice; matching a text to a child; linking writing and reading; balancing whole-class, group and individual teaching; and expert tutoring). He argued that these were equally crucial and equally deserving of attention.

In summary, children with language and communication needs require direct teaching in specific aspects of language, literacy and communication. However, they also benefit hugely from communication-friendly classrooms, in which it is acceptable to say "I don't understand"; and from teachers who are mindful of their own communication patterns, of their pupils' language and communication needs, and of the need to provide purposes and contexts for learning that motivate and support all children in using language and literacy to communicate.

References

Allington, R. L. (2005). The other five "pillars" of effective reading instruction. [President's message]. *Reading Today, 22*(6), 3.

Boyle, J., McCartney, E., Forbes, J., & O'Hare, A. (2007). A randomised controlled trial and economic evaluation of direct versus indirect and individual versus group modes of speech and language therapy for children with primary language impairment. *Health Technology Assessment, 11*(25), 1–158.

Conti-Ramsden, G., Durkin, K., Simkin, Z., & Knox, E. (2009). Specific language impairment and school outcomes 1: Identifying and explaining variability at the end of compulsory education. *International Journal of Language and Communication Disorders, 44*, 15–35.

Dollaghan, C., & Kaston, N. (1986). A comprehension monitoring program for language impaired children. *Journal of Speech and Hearing Disorders, 51*, 264–271.

Guthrie, J. T., & Humenick, N. M. (2004). Motivating students to read: Evidence for classroom practices that increase reading motivation. In P. McCardle & V. Chhabra (Eds.), *The voice of evidence in reading research* (pp. 329–355). New York: Erlbaum.

Guthrie, J. T., & Wigfield, A. (2000). Engagement and motivation in reading. In M. L. Kamil, P. B. Mosenthal, P. D. Pearson, & R. Barr (Eds.), *Handbook of reading research* (vol. 3, pp. 403–422). New York: Erlbaum.

Johnson, M. (2000, April). *Promoting understanding of the spoken word through active listening*. Paper presented at the conference of the National Association of Professionals Concerned with Language Impairment in Children (NAPLIC), University of Warwick, UK.

Law, J., Rush, R., Schoon, I., Parsons, S. (2009). Modelling developmental language difficulties from school entry into adulthood: Literacy, mental health and employment outcomes. *Journal of Speech, Language and Hearing Research, 52*, 1401–1416.

Learning and Teaching Scotland. (2000). *Support for learning: Part three, no 7: Developing the 5–14 curriculum for pupils with language and communication disorders*. Dundee: Author.

Learning and Teaching Scotland. (2010). *AiFL: Assessment is for learning: Self assessment toolkits: High quality interaction*. Retrieved 12 February 2010, from http://www.ltscotland.org.uk/assess/toolkit/earlyyears/highqualityinteractions.asp

Lee, W. (2008). *Speech, language and communication needs and primary school-aged children*. I CAN Talk Series, Issue 6. London: I CAN.

Lindsay, G., Dockrell, J., & Palikara, O. (in press). Self-esteem of adolescents with specific language impairment as they move from compulsory education. *International Journal of Language and Communication Disorders*, Early Online Article, 1–11. Posted online November 2009.

McCartney, E., Ellis, S., & Boyle, J. (2009). The mainstream primary school as a language-learning environment for children with language impairment: Implications of recent research. *Journal of Research in Special Education, 9*(2), 80–90.

McCartney, E., Ellis, S., Boyle, J., Turnbull, M., & Kerr, J. (in press). Developing a language support model for mainstream primary school teachers. *Child Language, Teaching and Therapy*.

Moss, G. (2007). *Literacy and gender*. Abingdon, England: Routledge.

Nash, M., & Donaldson, M. L. (2005). Word learning in children with vocabulary deficits. *Journal of Speech, Language and Hearing Research, 48*, 439–458.

National Institute of Child Health and Human Development. (2000). *Report of the National Reading Panel: Teaching children to read: An evidence-based assessment of the scientific research literature on reading and its implications for reading instruction* (NIH Publication No. 00-4769). Washington: US Government Printing Office

Stanovich, K. E. (1986). Matthew effects in reading: Some consequences of individual differences in the acquisition of literacy. *Reading Research Quarterly, 21*(4), 360–407.

CHAPTER 5
Phonological awareness: Motivating early literacy success

Gail Gillon and Brigid McNeill

Introduction

The strongest predictor of later reading success is early reading success. Simply put, success breeds success. It is critically important, therefore, that young children have positive early literacy experiences that will motivate them to attempt more challenging and advanced written language tasks as they mature through their school years (Hogan, Catts, & Little, 2005). This chapter focuses on the importance of phonological awareness to early word decoding and spelling development, particularly for children at risk for literacy difficulties. The chapter emphasises that through evidenced-based instruction and intervention practices it is possible for all children to reach their potential in early literacy development. The chapter is set within the context that both intrinsic and extrinsic variables will motivate young learners. Successful early word decoding experiences will begin a positive spiral of literacy learning in the home and school context that will serve to further motivate children to engage in reading and writing.

Our own motivation to focus on enhancing children's early reading success is strengthened by the United Nations' "Call for Action". We are in the last quarter of the United Nations Literacy Decade 2003–12, which is dedicated to global literacy. It is recognised at an international level that children from lower socioeconomic backgrounds or raised in poverty, children in rural and remote areas, children from indigenous populations and minority ethnic groups, and children with disabilities continue to underachieve in their literacy development. The United Nations is calling for urgent action, challenging us to mobilise our commitment to literacy and to reinforce more effective practices to ensure literacy achievement for *all* learners (Richmond, Robinson, & Sachs-Israel, 2008).

Phonological awareness

One instructional practice that has proven effective in motivating early reading success is phonological awareness. Children's awareness of the sound structure of words and their knowledge of how sounds in words relate to print influence their ability to decode and spell. A substantial body of research has demonstrated the vital importance of phonological awareness to early reading acquisition. Measures of phonological awareness at the phoneme level are powerful predictors of early reading achievement, particularly when combined with children's letter knowledge (see Gillon, 2004, for a review).

Phonological awareness is typically viewed as developing along a continuum, from being aware of larger linguistic units in words such as syllables, to onset rime units, and then to phonemes (Carroll, Snowling, Hulme, & Stevenson, 2003; Lonigan, Burgess, Anthony, & Barker, 1998). A range of assessment tools is available to assess young children's phonological awareness development (Gillon, 2004 provides examples of research-based assessment measures), including recent developments in computer-based assessments (e.g., Carsen, Gillon, & Boustead, 2009).

Many children will become aware of the sound structure of words through their early language experiences, such as engaging in nursery rhymes, shared book reading and vocabulary development. Some children, however, approach literacy instruction with very limited phonological awareness. Without specific intervention to facilitate this awareness, it is likely that these children will struggle in their early reading and spelling attempts. Perceived early failure can have a negative effect on a child's self-esteem and academic progress (Chapman &

Tunmer, 2003). This is likely to hamper their motivation to continue trying to achieve in a task they find difficult while observing their peers rapidly advancing their ability.

Phonological intervention strategies to motivate success

Phonological awareness interventions have proven successful in enhancing reading accuracy, reading comprehension and spelling (Ehri et al., 2001; see also National Reading Panel, n.d.). Phonological awareness intervention may also have a positive effect on word learning ability for children with specific language impairment (Zens, Gillon, & Moran, 2009). When children begin to experience success, coupled with extrinsic factors such as encouragement from teachers and parents, their motivation to further develop their skills will greatly increase (Morgan, Farkas, & Hibel, 2008). Thus, specific phonological awareness intervention can be viewed as an initial intrinsic motivator providing children with fundamental knowledge they require to access written language. It should be viewed within the context of a well-balanced classroom literacy programme that facilitates decoding and comprehension strategies to ensure fluent reading. Findings from research over the last two decades provide practitioners with clear guidelines as to the elements that will enhance the benefits of phonological awareness instruction for literacy. Gillon (2004) has described these elements, which are summarised below:

1. Phonological awareness instruction should focus on the phoneme level. For example, a programme might include activities that require the child to:
   - identify initial or final phonemes in words
   - segment words into phonemes
   - blend phonemes together to form words
   - manipulate phonemes in words to make new words.

   (See http://www.education.canterbury.ac.nz/people/gillon for free-to-download phonological awareness and other resources, and Gillon, 2006, for examples of programme content.)

2. Phonological awareness should be integrated with grapheme/phoneme knowledge, and the link between letters and sounds made explicit for the child.

3. Phonological awareness for children with very limited awareness may require more intensive instruction employing a small-group or individual intervention model.
4. Transfer of isolated phonological awareness skills to the reading and spelling process needs to be encouraged.

Based on these principles, phonological awareness intervention has produced encouraging results in terms of facilitating phonological awareness and early literacy success in a range of population groups that are at significant risk for persistent literacy difficulties. For example, in New Zealand, phonological awareness intervention has led to long-term gains in reading and spelling for preschool and school-aged children with moderate and severe spoken language impairment (Gillon 2000, 2002, 2005).

A multiple strategy framework

Motivating early literacy success for all children will require multiple strategies. Figure 1 depicts how the interlocking of a range of strategies may be necessary before we achieve early reading success for *all* children. Strategies related to the home and community, classroom or formal learning environment, specific interventions, preparation of teachers and teachers' professional learning, progress monitoring and research all need to be considered.

In the rest of this chapter we use this multiple strategy framework to consider phonological awareness as a motivator for literacy acquisition in differing contexts.

Home literacy strategy

Parents and caregivers play a critical role in motivating children to learn. A meta-analysis of 16 controlled intervention studies found that involving parents in reading activities with their child in the early school years has a positive impact on children's reading acquisition (a moderately large effect size of 0.65 was evident) (Senechal & Young, 2008). For this reason, the home literacy environment for children with disabilities requires careful consideration (e.g., see van Bysterveldt,

Figure 1 A multiple strategy framework

Gillon, & Foster-Cohen, in press). Children with disability may be less frequently engaged in home literacy activities compared to their peers without disabilities. Parents' expectations regarding their child's potential for literacy success may be lower, reducing extrinsic variables that motivate a young child to read. The findings from van Bysterveldt et al., (in press) and van Bysterveldt, Gillon, and Moran (2006) suggest that print referencing and phonological awareness strategies are useful for motivating preschool children with Down syndrome, and their parents, to more actively engage in learning during shared reading activities.

In this series of studies, parents were trained to bring their child's attention to print, initial phonemes in key words and the relationship between letters and sounds. For example, in reading the children's book *Spot* with their child, the parents would say:

This word says Spot [pointing to the printed word Spot].

Spot's name starts with a /s/ sound.

This is the letter s [pointing to the letter S in Spot's name].

It makes a /s/ sound.

Children were encouraged to articulate the sounds and key words as the parent pointed to the letter or word in print.

The socioeconomic impact on children's early reading development may stem from factors such as less exposure to literacy and less parental engagement with the child in language experiences that help facilitate early reading success. Lonigan and colleagues (1998) conducted a comprehensive study examining early phonological awareness development in young American children who attended preschool facilities. Remarkable differences in performance were evident between children in low- and middle-income environments as the children approached formal literacy instruction. Children from low socioeconomic backgrounds showed limited growth over time on syllable, rhyme and phoneme-level tasks compared to children from middle-income families. Figure 2 provides an illustrative interpretation of data reported in Lonigan et al.'s (1998) study on a measure of children's sensitivity to syllables in words.

Community strategy

It is important that communities and governments publically proclaim the importance of supporting young children in their reading development and present images and role models that will motivate children to read. Neuman and Celano (2006) examined the effectiveness of a community strategy to equalise access to library resources across low- and middle-income children in Philadelphia. The authors reported that although the strategy was successful in increasing library use for low-income children, differences in the quality of resource use remained. These results show the importance not only of improving access to literacy materials, but also of providing the appropriate education to ensure that improved use relates to real changes in literacy skills.

Figure 2 Syllable awareness development in children from low- and middle-income backgrounds

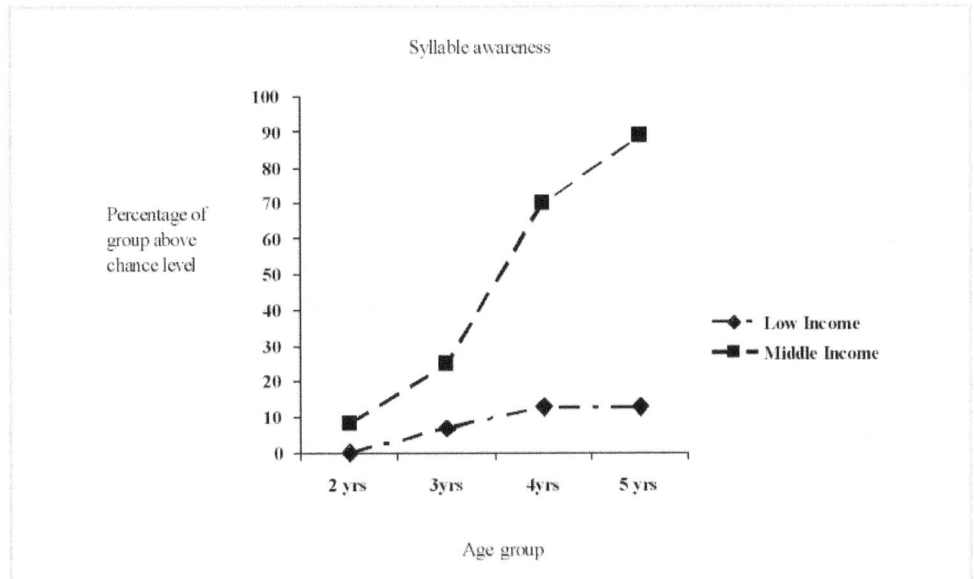

Teacher education strategy

Providers of initial teacher education are coming under increasing scrutiny in terms of their preparation of effective literacy teachers. Teachers' instructional literacy methods are crucial for motivating learning and facilitating early reading success. Recently, Joshi et al. (2009) examined the content of 17 textbooks that were widely adopted in university reading education classes for teachers across the US. The researchers evaluated the texts for evidence of information about the five critical components of literacy which the National Reading Panel recommends should be included in literacy instruction (phoneme awareness, phonics, fluency, vocabulary and text comprehension). Overall coverage of these components was variable, ranging from 4 percent to 60 percent. The coverage of phoneme awareness was particularly sparse, ranging from only 1 percent to 5 percent, and inaccurate information about phonological awareness development was noted. The research group concluded that many textbooks used in the preparation of teachers in literacy instruction do not provide adequate information regarding the fundamental elements of literacy instruction that will facilitate reading success.

Teachers' own phonological knowledge might also be compromised. Caroll and Gillon (2009) found that although specialist teachers of literacy demonstrated strong phonological knowledge, there was wide variability in performance among mainstream classroom teachers, student teachers and early childhood teachers. Academics in initial teacher education programmes need to ensure graduating teachers are well prepared to facilitate the fundamental language skills necessary for reading acquisition, including phonological awareness.

Classroom literacy strategy

There is a wide range of effective teaching strategies that motivate young children to strive for early reading success within the classroom context (Slavin, Lake, Chambers, Cheung, & Davis, 2009). To be motivated by a teacher's instruction, or inspired by the reflections of their peers during a lesson, children need to clearly hear speech within the classroom. The acoustic properties of classrooms can be very poor (Whitlock & Dodd, 2008), which will interfere with children's learning. This is particularly problematic for children who have fluctuating hearing loss, which is more common in lower socioeconomic environments and in some ethnic groups, including Māori and Pacific populations (see Good, 2010 for a review). A recent New Zealand study, which combined enhancing the listening environment of the classroom by installing a sound field amplification system and phonological awareness classroom-based instruction, proved effective in enhancing the children's phonological awareness knowledge (Good, Gillon, & Sockalingham, submitted). The participants in the study attended a Year 2 classroom in a school identified as being in a low socioeconomic area. The findings suggested that the children who benefited the most from the combined intervention were those who showed persistently poor phonological awareness knowledge prior to the beginning of the study.

Specific intervention strategy

Children at risk for literacy difficulties due to factors such as sensory impairments, speech and language disorders, and physical disabilities are likely to require specialist support to facilitate early reading success. It is critical that these interventions be evidence-based and motivate the learner to persist in literacy learning despite the challenges. An example of a phonologically based intervention that motivated children with severe speech disorder to succeed in both reading and spelling is provided below.

Twelve children with childhood apraxia of speech engaged in 18 hours of individual phonological awareness intervention with the second chapter author (see McNeill, Gillon, & Dodd, 2009a, 2009b for details). The improvement in spelling attempts for one boy in this study (see Figure 3) highlights this child's ability to rapidly change despite nearly three years of failing in literacy. The words illustrated in Figure 3 were selected from a wider writing sample. The pre-intervention attempt at the word "shark" was chosen because this represented one of the child's better attempts in the total sample, in that a more complex grapheme-phoneme connection (sh = two letters represented by one sound) was accurately represented. None of the

Figure 3 Pre- and post-phonological awareness intervention spelling attempts of a boy with childhood apraxia of speech aged 7 years 8 months at pre-intervention

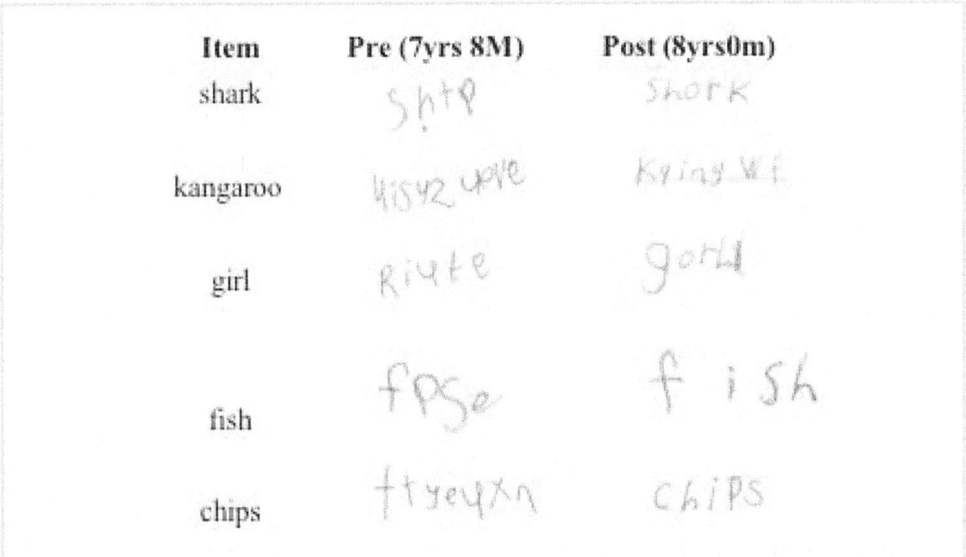

Item	Pre (7yrs 8M)	Post (8yrs0m)
shark	Shtp	Shork
kangaroo	Kis42 upre	Kring wf
girl	Riute	gorll
fish	fpSe	f i sh
chips	ttyeyxn	chips

Note: Items not directly trained in intervention

words were directly taught during the intervention period, and so improvements observed at post-intervention assessment suggest transfer of knowledge from the phonologically based intervention to a literacy task.

The post-intervention attempts show a relatively consistent relationship between the number of phonemes in the words and the graphemes represented within the spelling attempts, as well as improved letter–sound knowledge. This ability to "crack the code" gave the child an increased motivation to complete this spelling task in a more effortful manner at post-intervention. During the initial assessment he wrote random letters in a quick and haphazard fashion, whereas at follow-up assessment he strategically encoded each word using a sound-by-sound strategy, drawing on the skills gained in intervention.

Monitoring strategy

It is vital that strategies implemented to motivate young children's early reading success are monitored over time. If we are striving to ensure *all* children reach their potential in literacy achievement, careful monitoring of progress is required. Although a child experiencing early reading and writing difficulty may show accelerated gains in response to an effective teaching strategy, home programme or specific intervention, the maintenance of this progress and evidence of continued accelerated progress following the intervention need to be demonstrated or additional support provided. Share's (1995) self-teaching hypothesis of reading holds that successful early word decoding attempts will motivate increased engagement with print and new learning of more complex text. If phonological awareness interventions aim to facilitate early word decoding and spelling attempts, a successful outcome of the intervention will be ongoing independent decoding and encoding of print and the integration of phonological information with other strategies to facilitate word learning.

Well-structured monitoring assessments should provide teachers and parents with evidence of increasingly independent and more accurate word decoding and encoding abilities in the child's early literacy development. For early reading success to motivate children to attempt more advanced written language tasks, successful early reading experiences must be ongoing and cumulative.

Research strategy

At an international level, continued government resourcing of larger scale studies that investigate effective literacy practices is required. Increasingly, we are focused on what is working to motivate early reading success for all learners and reinforcing the widespread use of research-informed practices that have shown promise in experimental or quasi-experimental studies. Although literacy rates are rising, the United Nations has estimated that there are 774 million children and adults in the world who do not have adequate literacy skills, and this fact alone must motivate the research community to continue and to strengthen its efforts.

Summary

A child's awareness of the sound structure of words—that is, their phonological awareness knowledge—is a powerful predictor of early reading success. In turn, early reading success motivates children to engage in more advanced written language tasks, and a positive spiral effect from early reading success to later reading success and academic achievement begins. At a global level, however, children from clearly identified groups (such as children from lower socioeconomic backgrounds, indigenous populations and children with disabilities) do not experience this beginning cycle of success and are at risk of lowered motivation to engage with written language. For these children, a multiple-strategy approach that includes consideration of home, community, school, specific interventions, monitoring and research strategies may be necessary to ensure that early literacy success does indeed become a powerful motivator for all children.

References

Carroll, J., & Gillon, G. (2009, November). *Phonological awareness: What is the skill level of our educators?* Paper presented at the American-Speech-Language-Hearing Association (ASHA) annual convention, New Orleans.

Carroll, J. M., Snowling, M. J., Hulme, C., & Stevenson, J. (2003). The development of phonological awareness in preschool children. *Developmental Psychology, 39*(5), 913–923.

Carsen, K., Gillon, G., & Boustead, T. (2009, November). *The use of technologies in phonological awareness assessment: Pilot study*. Paper presented at the American-Speech-Language-Hearing Association (ASHA) annual convention, New Orleans.

Chapman, J. W., & Tunmer, W. E. (2003). Reading difficulties, reading-related self-perceptions, and strategies for overcoming negative self beliefs. *Reading and Writing Quarterly, 19*(1), 5–19.

Ehri, L. C., Nunes, S. R., Willows, D. M., Schuster, B. V., Yaghoub-Zadeh, Z., & Shanahan, T. (2001). Phonemic awareness instruction helps children learn to read: Evidence from the National Reading Panel's meta-analysis. *Reading Research Quarterly, 36*(3), 250–287.

Gillon, G. (2000). The efficacy of phonological awareness intervention for children with spoken language impairment. *Language, Speech, and Hearing Services in Schools, 31*, 126–141.

Gillon, G. (2005). Facilitating phoneme awareness development in 3- and 4-year-old children with speech impairment. *Language, Speech and Hearing Services in Schools, 36*(4), 308–324.

Gillon, G. (2006). Phonological awareness intervention: A preventive framework for preschool children with specific speech and language impairments. In R. J. McCauley & M. E. Fey (Eds.), *Treatment of language disorders in children: Conventional and controversial approaches* (pp. 279–307). Baltimore, MD: Paul H. Brookes.

Gillon, G. T. (2002). Follow-up study investigating benefits of phonological awareness intervention for children with spoken language impairment. *International Journal of Language and Communication Disorders, 37*(4), 381–400.

Gillon, G. T. (2004). *Phonological awareness: From research to practice*. New York: Guilford Press.

Good, V., Gillon, G., & Sockalingham, R. (submitted). *Enhancing phonological awareness in the classroom context*. Paper submitted for the 28th World Congress of the International Association of Logopedics and Phoniatrics (IALP), Athens.

Good, V. P. (2010). *An investigation of the effectiveness of integrating sound–field amplification and classroom-based phonological awareness intervention on the early reading development of young school children*. Unpublished thesis (Master of Audiology), University of Canterbury, Christchurch.

Hogan, T., Catts, H., & Little, T. (2005). The relationship between phonological awareness and reading: Implications for the assessment of phonological awareness. *Language, Speech, and Hearing Services in Schools, 36*, 285–293.

Joshi, R. M., Binks, E., Graham, L., Ocker-Dean, E., Smith, D. L., & Boulware-Gooden, R. (2009). Do textbooks used in university reading education courses conform to the instructional recommendations of the National Reading Panel? *Journal of Learning Disabilities, 42*(5), 458–463.

Lonigan, C., Burgess, S., Anthony, J. L., & Barker, T. A. (1998). Development of phonological sensitivity in 2- to 5-year-old children. *Journal of Educational Psychology, 90*(2), 294–311.

McNeill, B. C., Gillon, G. T., & Dodd, B. (2009a). The effectiveness of an integrated phonological awareness approach for children with childhood apraxia of speech (CAS). *Child Language Teaching and Therapy, 25*(3), 341–366.

McNeill, B. C., Gillon, G. T., & Dodd, B. (2009b). A longitudinal case study of the effects of an integrated phonological awareness program for identical twin boys with childhood apraxia of speech. *International Journal of Speech-Language Pathology, 11*(6), 482–495.

Morgan, P. L., Farkas, G., & Hibel, J. (2008). Matthew effects for whom? *Learning Disability Quarterly, 31*(4), 187–198.

National Reading Panel. (n.d.). *Teaching children to read: An evidence-based assessment of the scientific research literature on reading and its implications for reading instruction*. Retrieved from http:// www.nichd.nih.gov/ publications/nrp/upload/smallbook_pdf.pdf

Neuman, S. B., & Celano, D. (2006). The knowledge gap: Implications of leveling the playing field for low-income and middle-income children. *Reading Research Quarterly, 41*, 176–201.

Richmond, M., Robinson, C., & Sachs-Israel, M. (2008). *The global literacy challenge: A profile of youth and adult literacy at the mid-point of the United Nations Literacy Decade 2003–2012*. Paris: United Nations Educational Scientific and Cultural Organisation.

Senechal, M., & Young, L. (2008). The effect of family literacy interventions on children's acquisition of reading from kindergarten to grade 3: A meta-analytic review. *Review of Educational Research, 78*(4), 880–907.

Share, D. (1995). Phonological recoding and self-teaching: Sine qua non of reading acquisition. *Cognition, 55*, 151–218.

Slavin, R. E., Lake, C., Chambers, B., Cheung, A., & Davis, S. (2009). Effective reading programs for the elementary grades: A best-evidence synthesis. *Review of Educational Research, 79*(4), 1391–1466.

van Bysterveldt, A., Gillon, G. T., & Foster-Cohen, S. (in press). Literacy environments for children with Down syndrome: What's happening at home? *Down Syndrome Research and Practice*.

van Bysterveldt, A., Gillon, G. T., & Foster-Cohen, S. (in press). Integrated speech and phonological awareness intervention for pre-school children with Down syndrome. *International Journal of Language and Communication Disorders.*

van Bysterveldt, A. K., Gillon, G. T., & Moran, C. (2006). Enhancing phonological awareness and letter knowledge in preschool children with Down Syndrome. *International Journal of Disability, Development and Education, 53*(3), 301–329.

Whitlock, J. A. T., & Dodd, G. (2008). Speech intelligibility in classrooms: Specific acoustical needs for primary school children. *Building Acoustics, 15*(1), 35–47.

Zens, N. K., Gillon, G., & Moran, C. (2009). Effects of phonological awareness and semantic intervention on word-learning in children with specific language impairment. *International Journal of Speech–Language Pathology, 11*(6), 509–524.

CHAPTER 6
Motivating children with dyslexia

John Everatt and Gavin Reid

Introduction

This chapter covers some of the issues related to motivation and dyslexia. The discussion focuses on the consequences of learning difficulties that, in some children, manifest themselves in the form of negative affect, learnt helplessness and hence demotivation in educational settings. The chapter starts with a description of dyslexia. This is followed by a presentation of some of the evidence for the relationship between learning difficulties and negative emotion or motivational consequences. A discussion of some of the educational issues associated with dyslexia and perceived achievement follows in order to prime the reader for a brief practical implications section, which completes the chapter. Although all aspects of the relationships discussed cannot be covered here, we aim to provide the reader with an overview of some of the specific features that have been found to be associated with dyslexia.

Dyslexia: Characteristics and consequences

Dyslexia (sometimes called developmental dyslexia) typically refers to a problem with learning word-level literacy skills. Although this term is used around the world, "learning disabilities" has also been used to describe individuals with similar clusters of literacy learning difficulties. "Learning disabilities", however, would encompass individuals with other learning problems, such as difficulties with mathematics. The term "dyslexia" will therefore be used in this chapter, although data on learning disabilities will be reported where relevant to the discussion.

There are many differing views about dyslexia, but it has been described most consistently as occurring when reading and/or spelling develops incompletely or with great difficulty despite access to learning opportunities that are effective with most individuals, and as unexpected in relation to typical development in nonliteracy areas.[1] These literacy problems are most clearly demonstrated as a weakness in word decoding (i.e., translating between the written form and its verbal/spoken equivalent) and may stem from an underlying problem with phonological processing or the ability to process sounds within words efficiently (see also Gillon, 2004; Snowling, 2000; Stanovich, 1988). These word-level difficulties lead to problems with processing text that can have an impact on academic performance. As a result, a problem in basic word reading and spelling can lead ultimately to low educational qualifications that may produce poor employment opportunities.

These kinds of educational problems also have negative emotional or psychosocial consequences. Although they have been much less studied, these additional negative consequences of learning problems have been discussed for as long as educational learning difficulties themselves (see Critchley & Critchley, 1978). One of the main reasons for a lack of research in this area is the problem of disentangling the various variables that can affect a learner's performance. For example, environmental, personality and social factors can all influence learning (Mosley, 1996). This means there is a need to differentiate how students with

---

[1] See definitions by the British Dyslexia Association: http://www.bdadyslexia.org.uk/, the International Dyslexia Association: http://www.interdys.org/ and the New Zealand Ministry of Education: http://www.minedu.govt.nz/NZEducation.aspx, all retrieved January 2010.

dyslexia see themselves, both in general and, more specifically, as learners. Indeed, this complex reciprocal relationship between achievement, individual differences associated with affect and social/environmental influences, all of which can affect motivation (and hence learning and achievement), is a specific feature of work in this area and a relatively important aspect of this chapter.

It is also vital to appreciate (and remember) the diversity among individuals with dyslexia. Differences will exist in terms of the impact of dyslexia on achievement and the consequences that dyslexia has on the self and motivation.

Achievement, affect and control

Although there are differing views about self-esteem, typically it has been considered in terms of how closely an individual's perceived self matches their ideal self. Self-esteem has been linked to general self-concept, which includes behavioural, affective and cognitive appraisal of the self, and may be influenced by cultural factors that can determine the characteristics of the ideal self (Coopersmith, 1967). It has been postulated that academic self-esteem is vulnerable to underachievement from middle childhood, when the child becomes more aware of his or her successes and failures (Chapman, Silva, & Williams, 1984). Consistent with a relationship between educational failure and poor self-esteem, children with learning disabilities have been found to have lower self-esteem than their peers (Gjessing & Karlsen, 1989; Huntington & Bender, 1993; Rosenthal, 1973). In a review of studies reported between 1974 and 1986 on the relationship between learning disabilities and self-concept, Chapman (1988) concluded that children with learning disabilities were more likely than their normally achieving peers to view themselves negatively.

It can be argued that individuals with dyslexia may be poor appraisers of their own abilities, meaning that their perceived self may be further from their ideal self than their abilities should suggest. For example, McLoughlin, Fitzgibbon, and Young (1994) found that individuals with dyslexia had poor perceptions of their spelling abilities even though they may not have been as bad as they considered, and Butrowsky and Willows (1980) found that poor readers had low expectations of success not only in reading but also in drawing, which points to the poor self-worth feelings extending beyond the area of poor ability. Lawrence (1996) has argued that an individual's levels of achievement can be influenced by how they feel about themselves, suggesting a potential downwards spiral of poor achievement leading to poor self-esteem, which further affects performance. Equally, good self-awareness has been considered a factor in a successful adult life for the individual with a learning problem (Goldberg, Higgins, Raskind, & Herman, 2003).

Self-awareness may also be related to feelings of being in control. Chan (1994) compared students with and without a disability and looked at the relationship between motivation and strategic learning. She found a pattern of learnt helplessness: feelings of having no control of their lives was observed among many poor learners. When children with a learning difficulty experience failure, they may not look for internal factors, such as ability and effort, but rather external controls, such as luck, which may affect achievement motivation (Oka & Paris, 1987). Indeed, Mruk (1990) has proposed that positive levels of self-esteem are linked with having an internal sense of control, which increases an individual's motivation and achievement in the learning situation.

Consistent with this potential relationship, Margerison's (1996) work has identified an association between self-esteem and locus of control in children with emotional problems, and Humphrey and Mullins (2002) have argued from their data that dyslexic children are more likely to attribute success to external factors, such as the teacher, rather than to their own ability, which, as discussed above, may lead to feelings of learnt helplessness. Although being given a difficult task can be motivating, it is rare to find continued motivation to succeed when only failure is experienced. Typically, continued failure leads to demotivation and feelings of helplessness.

The relationship between control and success has been studied in a small number of studies focusing on children with learning disabilities/dyslexia. Gerber, Ginsberg, and Reiff (1992) studied a group of highly successful adults with learning disabilities and considered factors such as the individual's desire to achieve (an internal factor) and adaptations to the environment (an external factor). The researchers argued that control was a key to success. The higher the internal and external control, the more likely an individual was to take control of their life and the higher was their ability to adjust to their disability and succeed in life. The work of Burden (Burden, 2005; Burden & Burdett, 2007) has identified a relationship between improved academic performance and confidence (in terms of predicating success on a task) and personal control. These data were derived from work in a specialist school that produced positive attitudes towards learning, suggesting that being educated in an environment with a strong internalising focus may result in positive learning outcomes. A study by Everatt, Al-Azmi, Al-Sharhan, and Elbeheri (submitted) investigated academic poor achievement indicative of learning disabilities among Arabic children and found that low self-esteem was characteristic of those with a poor level of literacy, although this was moderated by locus of control.

Overall, such findings with children and adults suggest that feelings of control may be related to overcoming negative emotional consequences and improve success both within and outside educational contexts.

Achievement and motivation

Achievement, and the demotivating effects of lack of achievement, is influenced by the perception of the individual; for example, perceptions of the importance of literacy and/or mathematics, and school in general, can influence the relationship between academic performance and negative affect (see Hettinger, 1982). Indeed, it can be quite illuminating talking to a group of high achievers. Some very successful learners are not aware of their own success. They may measure or perceive success in a different way from others. A student who is accustomed to obtaining straight As may feel a failure if she/he obtains a B, yet this can be a highly commendable grade. The "must be best" syndrome is quite widespread in today's competitive society, and although this has some positive elements, it can be seen as one that can place enormous pressure on the learner.

The key point here is what do we mean by "achievement"? Achievement is not necessarily simply reaching the goal set by the teacher. Achievement depends on the learner and their readiness for the task. If a person does not achieve, the task will need to be revised until they can achieve it. Motivation is related to what the learner has already achieved, and this needs to be linked to current and future learning.

Strategies for maintaining motivation

For many students with dyslexia the sight—or indeed the thought—of certain types of tasks can be sufficient to demotivate them. This places an onus on teachers to develop achievable tasks that can sustain motivation. This can be the first major barrier that has to be overcome in order to maintain motivation. Some learners who have experienced repeated failure will become totally demotivated and will not want to engage in learning new material in any way at all. It is important that children can experience success before they become demotivated. It is for this reason that great care must be taken when developing tasks to ensure they are motivating and—even more importantly—the learner believes the task is achievable. Breaking a task down into small steps, with every step representing an achievable and rewarding outcome for the learner, can be both rewarding and motivating. (For further details about such strategies, see Reid, 2007.)

Although rewards are useful, they should be seen as a short-term strategy—a step towards self-motivation. Rewards are normally only successful in the short term and can help children who need a boost, particularly if they are finding the task challenging. Rewards must also be achievable, and the learner must value the reward. Ideally it is best if the reward is negotiated with the learner. This needs to be considered carefully in terms of the feedback given to the child who may be struggling. Every learner needs feedback to ensure he/she is on the correct path. However, feedback is often used as a means of grading or correcting. In using feedback this way the teacher runs the risk of demotivating the learner. It is important that feedback is seen as different from correcting work, particularly for the child with a difficulty. Feedback should be continuous and formative and not necessarily come at the end of a task. Feedback should also be positive or framed in a positive manner. Clearly, rewards and feedback can be dealt with separately, but giving rewards at the same time as negative feedback may be at best confusing, and more likely self-defeating.

It is also important to consider the complete learning experience and appreciate the importance of the environment (Reid, 2007). Social interaction can be beneficial for learners with dyslexia because it can help develop important social skills, such as turn taking and sharing, and listening to other people's opinions. The process of helping and working with others can in itself be motivating. Group dynamics can be positive or negative, however, and it is important to ensure that the composition of the group is beneficial to all. A constructive and positive group working harmoniously can be a significant motivator. A motivated group will be able to pool the resources of all the members of the group, and this can be a strong motivating force.

In fact one can take this a step further and focus not on the individual student but on the notion of the motivated school. School ethos, school culture and school climate are important factors that can promote a healthy school (Dunham, 1995; Killick, 2005; McLean, 2004). And a healthy school can provide the supportive learning environment that is required by students who are vulnerable to demotivation and failure.

Intervention, affect and motivation

Both motivation and achievement are influenced by many factors. In the child who is struggling to achieve expected levels of performance this relationship can be just as complex, though the link from low achievement to poor affect, low self-concept, loss of control and feelings of helplessness can culminate in demotivation that negatively influences achievement. This spiral of negative consequences will need to be overcome in many children with dyslexia for learning interventions to show success. Miles (2004) believes that if a child overcomes his or her learning difficulties early in school, this will increase confidence, allowing the individual to better cope with pressures in later life. However, a child who does not overcome his/her disability will experience higher stress levels, causing them to undermine their motivation, which can lead to consequences in the child's educational development.

Lewis (1984) found that a structured group-counselling programme improved reading achievement, as well as self-concept, among elementary school children, and similar effects may be apparent for children with learning difficulties, particularly those in middle school (see a review by Elbaum & Vaughn, 2001). This argues for a combined educational and psychological response, particularly for older children who may have developed negative feelings of self-worth following failure in educational achievement, which may be coupled with demotivation. However, strategies targeted at improving self-esteem and feelings of control may be implemented best once gains in achievement have started and are likely to continue. If gains in achievement are short-lived or perceived as external to the individual, there is likely to be little effect on self-concept or on motivation.

For example, strategies that build on strengths have been found to have positive effects on educational achievement in older children with learning disabilities, whereas trying to remediate areas of weakness has been less effective (see Weeks, Brooks, & Everatt, 2002). Clearly, further work is necessary, but this strategic combined approach may prove useful, particularly for older children with learning disabilities who have experienced a prolonged period of failure during their education. Building positive self-concept through achievable goals (and potentially good counselling support) will improve motivation and enhance the positive effects of interventions targeted at improving literacy among individuals with dyslexia. Ignoring these influences of negative affect and demotivation will reduce the likelihood of an intervention's success.

Implications for practice

Two general implications follow from this brief review. The first is the need to attempt to avoid/reduce learning difficulties and their consequent negative emotion/motivation through appropriate teaching methods and learning environments. Well-trained teachers (particularly those working in early learning contexts, such as the first year or two of formal learning), who are equipped to deal with a diversity of learners, including those with special teaching needs, and who are schooled in up-to-date teaching methods, are the most effective response to reduce the negative relationships discussed in this chapter. For example, early phoneme awareness and letter–sound training can reduce the subsequent incidence of literacy-learning problems associated with dyslexia (Elbro & Petersen, 2004), and interventions based on similar themes show good outcomes when implemented early in literacy learning (Torgesen, 2005).

The second implication is that if learning problems are not recognised early enough, then interventions will need to focus much more on the whole person (i.e., the causes and consequences of the learning difficulty, as well as the developing differences between individuals that will influence the manifestation of difficulties and the success of interventions) rather than on literacy alone. The evidence indicates that, even with older children with dyslexia, interventions such as the phonological awareness and phonological decoding training referred to above can be successful (Gillon, 2004). However, a range of tools will be needed to support learning and allow access to the curriculum. Above all, motivation will need to be maintained by allowing the child with special needs to do things they are good at and enjoy, although literacy learning can be integrated into many areas, including play, sport, art, drama and music. Special-needs teacher training, as well as teams of additionally qualified professionals working with the normal classroom teachers, will be needed to develop, and implement, such a range of tools if education is to become a truly inclusive system.

References

Burden, R. L. (2005). *Dyslexia and self-concept: Seeking a dyslexic identity*. London: Whurr.

Burden, R. L., & Burdett, J. (2007). What's in a name? Students with dyslexia: Their use of metaphor in making sense of their disability. *British Journal of Special Education, 34*, 77–81.

Butrowsky, I. S., & Willows, D. M. (1980). Cognitive-motivational characteristics of children varying in reading ability: Evidence for learned helplessness in poor readers. *Journal of Educational Psychology, 72*, 408–422.

Chan, L. K. S. (1994). Relationship of motivation, strategic learning, and reading achievement in grades 5, 7, and 9. *Journal of Experimental Education, 62*, 319–339.

Chapman, J. (1988). Learning disabled children's self-concepts. *Review of Educational Research, 58*, 347–371.

Chapman, J. W., Silva, P., & Williams, S. (1984). Academic self-concept: Some developmental and emotional correlates in nine year old children. *British Journal of Educational Psychology, 54*, 284–292.

Coopersmith, S. A. (1967). *The antecedents of self-esteem*. San Francisco: Freeman.

Critchley, M., & Critchley, E. A. (1978). *Dyslexia defined*. London: Acford.

Dunham, J. (1995). *Developing effective school management*. London: Routledge.

Elbaum, B., & Vaughn, S. (2001). School-based interventions to enhance the self-concept of students with learning disabilities: A meta-analysis. *Elementary School Journal, 101,* 303–329.

Elbro, C., & Petersen, D. K. (2004). Long-term effects of phoneme awareness and letter sound training: An intervention study with children at risk for dyslexia. *Journal of Educational Psychology, 96,* 660–670.

Everatt, J., Al-Azmi, Y., Al-Sharhan, A., & Elbeheri, G. (submitted). *Emotion and educational achievement in Arabic children.*

Gerber, P. J., Ginsberg, R., & Reiff, H. B. (1992). Identifying alterable patterns in employment success for highly successful adults with learning disabilities. *Journal of Learning Disabilities, 8,* 475–487.

Gillon, G. T. (2004). *Phonological awareness: From research to practice.* New York: Guilford Press.

Gjessing, H. J., & Karlsen, B. (1989). *A longitudinal study of dyslexia.* New York: Springer.

Goldberg, R., Higgins, E., Raskind, M., & Herman, K. (2003). Predictors of success in individuals with learning disabilities: A qualitative analysis of a 20 year longitudinal study. *Learning Disabilities Research and Practice, 18,* 222–236.

Hettinger, C. (1982). The impact of reading deficiency on the global self concept of the adolescent. *Journal of Early Adolescence, 2,* 293–300.

Humphrey, N., & Mullins, P. M. (2002). Personal constructs and attribution for academic success and failure in dyslexia. *British Journal of Special Education, 29,* 196–203.

Huntington, D. D., & Bender, W. N. (1993). Adolescents with learning disabilities at risk? Emotional well-being, depression, suicide. *Journal of Learning Disabilities, 26,* 159–166.

Killick, S. (2005). *Emotional literacy—at the heart of the school ethos.* London: Paul Chapman.

Lawrence, D. (1996). *Enhancing self-esteem in the classroom.* London: Paul Chapman.

Lewis, H. W. (1984). A structured group counseling program for reading disabled elementary students. *School Counselor, 31,* 454–459.

Margerison, A. (1996). Self-esteem: Its effect on the development and learning of children with EBD. *Support for Learning, 11,* 176–180.

McLean, A. (2004). *The motivated school.* London: Sage.

McLoughlin, D., Fitzgibbon, G., & Young, V. (1994). *Adult dyslexia: Assessment, counselling and training.* London: Whurr.

Miles, T. R. (Ed.). (2004). *Dyslexia and stress* (2nd ed.). London: Whurr.

Mosley, J. (1996). *Quality circle time in the primary classroom.* Cambridge: LDA.

Mruk, C. (1990). *Self-esteem: Research, theory and practice.* London: Free Association.

Oka, E. R., & Paris, S. G. (1987). Patterns of motivation and reading skills in under-achieving children. In S. J. Ceci (Ed.), *Handbook of cognitive, social and neurological aspects of learning disabilities* (Vol II) (pp. 15–146). Hillsdale, NJ: LEA.

Reid, G. (2007). *Motivating learners in the classroom: Ideas and strategies.* London: Sage.

Rosenthal, J. H. (1973). Self esteem in dyslexic children. *Academic Therapy, 9,* 27–39.

Snowling, M. J. (2000). *Dyslexia* (2nd ed.). Oxford: Blackwell.

Stanovich, K. E. (1988). Explaining the differences between the dyslexic and the garden variety poor reader: The phonological-core variable difference model. *Journal of Learning Disabilities, 21,* 590–604.

Torgesen, J. K. (2005). Recent discoveries on remedial interventions for children with dyslexia. In M. J. Snowling & C. Hulme (Eds.), *The science of reading: A handbook* (pp. 521–537). Malden, MA: Blackwell.

Weeks, S., Brooks, P., & Everatt, J. (2002). Differences in learning to spell: Relationships between cognitive profiles and learning responses to teaching methods. *Educational and Child Psychology, 19,* 47–62.

CHAPTER 7

Fostering story comprehension: Motivating struggling readers to engage in literature-based activities

Marleen F. Westerveld

Introduction

The ultimate goal of learning to read is undeniably to understand what is written. For successful understanding of written texts children rely on a range of skills, including word decoding and spoken language comprehension, as well as motivational variables (Chapman, Tunmer, & Prochnow, 2000; Morgan, Fuchs, Compton, Cordray, & Fuchs, 2008; Taboada, Tonks, Wigfield, & Guthrie, 2009). It is well known that poor readers in general are less motivated to read (Chapman et al., 2000). This is concerning, because reduced reading exposure, especially to more complex reading materials, will not only affect achievement in reading-related tasks, but may also constrain spoken language development in the areas of advanced morphology, syntax and vocabulary (e.g., Echols, West, Stanovich, & Zehr, 1996). This chapter focuses on the importance of one aspect of spoken language comprehension that many poor readers struggle with: story comprehension. It argues that improving children's story comprehension ability through narrative text structure intervention will help foster an enjoyment of stories, with the ultimate aim of enhancing motivation for reading (e.g., Sonnenschein & Munsterman, 2002).

Spoken language comprehension

Spoken language comprehension can be defined as the process by which meaning is extracted from words, sentences and discourses. When children start learning to read, the reading materials are often simple and do not challenge or extend their spoken language comprehension skills. As a result, during the initial stages of reading acquisition the link between spoken language comprehension and reading comprehension is rather weak. This changes as children become more proficient readers. By the time children reach the upper primary school level, spoken language comprehension has a strong link with reading comprehension (Catts, Hogan, & Adlof, 2005). Overall, research suggests that between 33 percent and 50 percent of the poor readers we encounter in our school system show weaknesses in spoken language comprehension (e.g., Catts, Hogan, & Fey, 2003; Tunmer & Chapman, 2007). Although spoken language comprehension can be assessed at the word, sentence and text level, the focus of this chapter is on text-level comprehension of one particular narrative genre: fictional stories. During the early school years children encounter fictional stories on a daily basis, such as during shared reading, in homework reading activities or when reading independently for pleasure.

To successfully understand a spoken or written story, children need adequate spoken language skills at the word and sentence level, and they rely on activation of background knowledge in long-term memory, including world knowledge and narrative text structure knowledge. Constructionist theories hold that children build a "mental model" of a situation depicted in a story (e.g., Graesser, Singer, & Trabasso, 1994). Narrative text structure knowledge, in particular, provides a child with expectations about the generic make-up of a story, which improves the clarity of the mental model and helps the child to identify the key points, thus facilitating both comprehension and memory of that story. Without adequate narrative text structure knowledge a story might be perceived as a collection of unrelated events, undoubtedly impeding the enjoyment of fictional stories in general. Seminal work by Stein and Glenn (1979) proposed that most problem-oriented stories contain setting information, characters, a problem, a plan, actions (to try to solve the problem), resolution and conclusion. In addition, many fictional stories represent another level of meaning that goes beyond the plot. This is referred to as the theme, or the concept that holds the story together. This concept may consist of a lesson (e.g., "We should always try our hardest") or an observation (e.g., "Some people will end up in hospital when they get sick") (Williams, 2002). Previous research has indicated the difficulties children with reading problems can have with narrative text structure knowledge (e.g., Cain, Oakhill, & Bryant, 2004). The next section will consider ways in which to assess story comprehension and narrative text structure knowledge in young primary school-aged children.

Assessment of story comprehension and narrative text structure knowledge

Given the importance of story comprehension ability to the reading comprehension process, especially during the early school years, it is surprising that there are few assessments available that adequately identify these difficulties in poor readers and that can be used repeatedly to measure change as a result of either typical reading tuition or more specific intervention (Catts et al., 2005). To get an indication of children's text structure knowledge, a spoken story comprehension task can be used in which a child is asked questions that tap underlying narrative text structure components. This type of task was used in our own two-year longitudinal study, in which 14 children with a mixed reading disability profile (i.e., both word decoding and oral language comprehension difficulties contributed to their reading comprehension problems) were seen on three separate occasions, approximately eight months apart (Westerveld, Gillon, & Moran, 2008). The children were asked to answer 10 story comprehension questions (different stories were used at each assessment) after listening to a fictional story.

When comparing their performance to that of a group of carefully matched peers with typical reading skills, it was found that they scored persistently lower over the two-year period. These results not only indicate that the story comprehension task was sensitive to reading ability, but also that mere exposure to fictional stories in a classroom context was not enough to accelerate the story comprehension skills of these struggling readers. To determine the clinical usefulness of this type of story comprehension task with young primary school-aged children, a field study was conducted with typically developing children attending mainstream primary schools in New Zealand.

The field study

Sixty-four typically developing New Zealand children aged between 6 years 0 months and 7 years 11 months, who attended Year 2 (n = 24) or Year 3 (n = 40) of their local primary schools in suburban Auckland, participated in this exploratory study. The schools were categorised as having mid-socioeconomic status based on the Ministry of Education ranking system. These children had no known history of hearing disorder, neurological disorder or speech–language disorders that required intervention, spoke English as their first language and were progressing normally at school. There were 28 boys and 36 girls from NZ European (73.4 percent), Māori (14.1 percent), Pasifika (7.8 percent) and "other" (4.7 percent) ethnic backgrounds.

All children were seen individually and listened to the story *Frog Goes to Dinner* on tape while looking at the pictures in a wordless 30-page picture book (Mayer, 1974). The story is about a little boy's pet frog, which escapes from the boy's pocket in a fancy restaurant and wreaks havoc for all involved. Afterwards the children were asked 10 comprehension questions that tapped underlying text structure elements as well the overall theme of the story. For example, "Who was the story about?" (main character/s), "How did the people who were playing music or dining at the restaurant feel about seeing a frog in the restaurant?" (problem), "What happened at the end of the story?" (conclusion) and "What would be another good name for this story?" (theme).

Analysis of the results from this field study showed no differences in performance on the story comprehension task between Year 2 and Year 3 children. These results imply that story comprehension ability as measured in this task is not sensitive to age or year of schooling, but may be a skill that relies on the presence or absence of narrative text structure knowledge in long-term memory. When analysing the results as one group, there was a relatively normal distribution, indicating that the task had no floor or ceiling effects. When calculating percentiles (see Table 1), based on weighted averages, the results indicated that children who answered four or fewer questions correctly performed in the bottom 10 percent (i.e., 90 percent of the children performed better), whereas children who answered eight or more questions correctly performed in the top 10 percent.

Table 1 Distributional performance and statistics on the story comprehension measure

Mean	Median	SD	5%	10%	25%	50%	75%	90%	95%	Skewness	Kurtosis
6.3	6.0	1.5	4.00	4.00	5.00	6.00	7.00	8.00	9.00	-.269	.175

Notes: Performance is displayed as number of questions correct out of 10. SD = standard deviation. The closer the skewness (shape of the distribution) and kurtosis (peakedness) statistics are to 0, the more normal the distribution.

Although these initial findings are promising, more research is required to determine the sensitivity of such a task for identifying story comprehension difficulties in poor readers. Future research should also investigate if a link exists between poor performance on this story comprehension task and a child's motivation to engage in stories. It could be hypothesised that children with poor story comprehension skills may be less likely to enjoy stories and hence be less motivated to engage in tasks that involve fictional stories; for example, during instructional reading, shared reading and independent reading. Until such time, the story comprehension task described here can potentially be used in a classroom setting by adapting the content of the questions so that they tap into the narrative text structure elements of other fictional stories. This may help to identify those children whose poor story comprehension skills contribute to their reading comprehension difficulties. These children would benefit from focused narrative structure intervention, which would help motivate an engagement in story-related reading and writing tasks.

Intervention

To determine whether narrative text structure intervention is effective for enhancing children's story comprehension skills, Westerveld and Gillon (2008a) conducted an intervention study that specifically addressed children's text structure knowledge. Ten children who had participated in the longitudinal investigation of poor readers described above (Westerveld et al., 2008) attended 12 twice-weekly group sessions. The use of small groups rather than one-to-one instruction was a way of motivating children to attend, share their experiences and learn from each other. It was interesting to note that a high percentage of these children told the author that they did not like reading, and some children were initially reluctant to attend the group sessions. By week 3, however, most of the children looked forward to attending and were active group participants.

Based on available best-practice evidence (e.g., Gersten, Fuchs, Williams, & Baker, 2001), and incorporating many of the motivational mechanisms identified by Pressley and colleagues (Pressley, 2003; Pressley, Gaskins, Solic, & Collings, 2006), the intervention contained the following key aspects:

1. use of high-quality children's literature that contained a well-defined story structure and a literate style of language (see Westby, 2005), which appealed to seven- to nine-year-old children and was short enough to discuss in one 50-minute session
2. use of graphic organisers, such as narrative text structure charts and laminated text structure labels
3. use of the "go meta" principle (see Paul, 2007), whereby: children were encouraged to think and talk about stories; it was explained to the children that "good" stories contain all eight story structure elements; and the children were taught to "think out aloud" when analysing stories and to provide each other with feedback following the retelling of stories (collaborative learning)
4. use of instructional scaffolding to help the children analyse stories and retell the stories.

Results clearly indicated that the narrative structure intervention programme was effective for enhancing these children's story comprehension skills (Westerveld & Gillon, 2008a). Moreover, these improvements in story comprehension were sustained over time (Westerveld & Gillon, 2007). Considering that these children had demonstrated persistent difficulties in story comprehension prior to the intervention, the results showed that systematic focused explicit group intervention was needed to accelerate these poor readers' story comprehension skills. Enhanced story comprehension will help support these children's ongoing reading (comprehension) development, and will increase their motivation to engage in stories, in both written and spoken formats.

When investigating the performance of one of the children (Danielle) in the intervention study in more detail, an interesting finding emerged (Westerveld & Gillon, 2008b). Following the narrative text structure intervention, Danielle made significant progress on a measure of expressive vocabulary (in a story retelling task). Two possible explanations for this improvement were proposed. First, repeated exposures to stories is known to improve vocabulary skills (Penno, Wilkinson, & Moore, 2002), so it is possible that the frequent reading of story books during the intervention was sufficient to enhance Danielle's vocabulary skills. Second, with improved text structure knowledge, fewer cognitive resources are needed to grasp the overall meaning of the story, which means that more resources are available to focus on individual words in a story and derive their meaning from the context (see also Graesser et al., 1994). More research in this area is needed, but the benefits of motivating children with poor reading skills to engage in well-formed children's literature are evident.

Summary

Although it is unclear to what extent reading motivation, reading comprehension ability and spoken language skills overlap, the serious long-term implications of difficulties in spoken language and/or reading ability have been well defined, and the importance of instigating appropriate interventions is obvious. Appreciating the importance of story comprehension ability for successful engagement in many reading-related tasks is essential. Story comprehension difficulties in poor readers can be identified by asking the child questions relating to underlying narrative text structure components, following exposure to a spoken story. Motivating those poor readers who show story comprehension weaknesses to engage in stories is critical, because poor understanding of narrative texts will undeniably affect children's enjoyment of tasks that involve either written or spoken stories, such as shared reading or independent reading for pleasure. To help motivate these struggling readers and improve their attitudes towards reading, evidence-based focused small-group intervention aimed at enhancing their knowledge of narrative text structures may be necessary.

References

Cain, K., Oakhill, J., & Bryant, P. (2004). Children's reading comprehension ability: Concurrent prediction by working memory, verbal ability, and component skills. *Journal of Educational Psychology, 96*(1), 31–42.

Catts, H. W., Hogan, T. P., & Adlof, S. M. (2005). Developmental changes in reading and reading disabilities. In H. W. Catts & A. G. Kamhi (Eds.), *Connections between language and reading disabilities* (pp. 25–40). Mahwah, NJ: Lawrence Erlbaum.

Catts, H. W., Hogan, T. P., & Fey, M. E. (2003). Subgrouping poor readers on the basis of individual differences in reading-related abilities. *Journal of Learning Disabilities, 36*(2), 151–164.

Chapman, J. W., Tunmer, W. E., & Prochnow, J. E. (2000). Early reading-related skills and performance, reading self-concept, and the development of academic self-concept: A longitudinal study. *Journal of Educational Psychology, 92*(4), 703–708.

Echols, L. D., West, R. F., Stanovich, K. E., & Zehr, K. S. (1996). Using children's literacy activities to predict growth in verbal cognitive skills: A longitudinal investigation. *Journal of Educational Psychology, 88*(2), 296–304.

Gersten, R., Fuchs, L. S., Williams, J. P., & Baker, S. (2001). Teaching reading comprehension strategies to students with learning disabilities: A review of research. *Review of Educational Research, 71*(2), 279–320.

Graesser, A. C., Singer, M., & Trabasso, T. (1994). Constructing inferences during narrative text comprehension. *Psychological Review, 101*(3), 371–395.

Mayer, M. (1974). *Frog goes to dinner*. New York: Penguin Young Readers Group.

Morgan, P. L., Fuchs, D., Compton, D., L., Cordray, D. S., & Fuchs, L. S. (2008). Does early reading failure decrease children's reading motivation? *Journal of Learning Disabilities, 41*(5), 387–404.

Paul, R. (2007). *Language disorders from infancy through adolescence: Assessment and Intervention* (3rd ed.). Baltimore, MD: Mosby Elsevier.

Penno, J. F., Wilkinson, I. A. G., & Moore, D. W. (2002). Vocabulary acquisition from teacher explanation and repeated listening to stories: Do they overcome the Matthew effect? *Journal of Educational Psychology, 94*(1), 23–33.

Pressley, M. (2003). Introduction to the many motivational mechanisms in education. In M. Pressley, S. E. Dolezal, L. M. Raphael, L. Mohan, A. D. Roehrig, & K. Bogner (Eds.), *Motivating primary-grade students* (pp. 1–30). New York: Guilford Press.

Pressley, M., Gaskins, I. W., Solic, K., & Collings, S. (2006). A portrait of a benchmark school: How a school produces high achievement in students who previously failed. *Journal of Educational Psychology, 98*(2), 282–306. DOI: 10.1037/0022-0663.98.2.282

Sonnenschein, S., & Munsterman, K. (2002). The influence of home-based reading interactions on 5-year-olds' reading motivations and early literacy development. *Early Childhood Research Quarterly, 17*(3), 318–337.

Stein, N., & Glenn, C. (1979). An analysis of story comprehension in elementary school children. In R. O. Freedle (Ed.), *New directions in discourse processing* (Vol. 2, pp. 53–120). Norwood, NJ: Ablex.

Taboada, A., Tonks, S., Wigfield, A., & Guthrie, J. (2009). Effects of motivational and cognitive variables on reading comprehension. *Reading and Writing, 22*(1), 85–106.

Tunmer, W. E., & Chapman, J. W. (2007). Language-related differences between discrepancy-defined and non-discrepancy-defined poor readers: A longitudinal study of dyslexia in New Zealand. *Dyslexia, 13*, 42–66.

Westby, C. E. (2005). Assessing and remediating text comprehension problems. In H. W. Catts & A. G. Kamhi (Eds.), *Language and reading disabilities* (2nd ed., pp. 157–232). Boston: Pearson Education.

Westerveld, M. F., & Gillon, G. T. (2007, May). *A follow-up study examining the effectiveness of oral narrative intervention for children with mixed reading disability*. Paper presented at the Speech Pathology Australia national conference: A Different Perspective, Sydney.

Westerveld, M. F., & Gillon, G. T. (2008a). Oral narrative intervention for children with mixed reading disability. *Child Language Teaching and Therapy, 24*(1), 31–54.

Westerveld, M. F., & Gillon, G. T. (2008b). Story structure intervention for a child with mixed reading disability: A developmental case study. *New Zealand Journal of Speech–Language Therapy, 63*, 45–56.

Westerveld, M. F., Gillon, G. T., & Moran, C. (2008). A longitudinal investigation of oral narrative skills in children with mixed reading disability. *International Journal of Speech–Language Pathology, 10*(3), 132–145.

Williams, J. P. (2002). Using the theme scheme to improve story comprehension. In C. C. Block & M. Pressley (Eds.), *Comprehension instruction: Research-based best practices* (pp. 126–139). New York: Guilford Press.

CHAPTER 8
Motivating Māori students in literacy learning: Listening to culture

Angus Hikairo Macfarlane

Introduction

How best to serve a culturally diverse student body has been a topic of intensive policy focus and development for many decades. Throughout this time a raft of far-reaching policies, national strategies and theoretical models have been proposed, targeted at enhancing the quality of educational practice and creating a more culturally responsive education system. This continued attention stems from a growing awareness that many current educational processes are not working as well for a large and growing percentage of the student body; indeed, it appears that this disparity is now becoming entrenched. In New Zealand, the sub-group of school students who are being severely affected by this unacceptable variance are Māori (the indigenous people of Aotearoa New Zealand), who are dropping out of school at twice or three times the rate of their non-Māori counterparts (Ministry of Education, 2008).

Students and their cultures need to be at the centre of teaching and literacy learning. When teachers have a knowledge of and empathy for Māori culture, language and tikanga, and introduce texts that include authentic Māori perspectives, they are more likely to provide an environment that motivates Māori students in their literacy learning (Ministry of Education, 2006). Successful teachers acknowledge, respect and build on the beliefs and experiences that all students bring with them to classrooms. By affirming and valuing students' cultures, a culturally responsive teacher can make a significant difference to the educational outcomes of any student at risk of experiencing educational failure. This chapter examines how teachers' attitudes, expectations and approaches to teaching have a significant impact on motivation and achievement in literacy learning, and learning in general, for students from culturally diverse backgrounds.

The New Zealand context

Within the New Zealand context, student achievement data suggest that many Māori students are underperforming relative to their potential, despite the fact that there have been concerted efforts directed at improving the achievement of this group (Gillon & Macfarlane, 2009; Glynn, Otrel-Cass, Cowie, & Macfarlane, 2008). The two main objectives of these efforts have been to enhance the educational achievement of Māori students and to improve the pedagogical practices of teachers, regardless of their (the teachers') ethnicities.

There is, it would appear, cautious but moderate acceptance by providers and consumers of education in New Zealand that effective and authentic services in Māori education are on the rise. A revised national curriculum (Ministry of Education, 2007) and a new national strategy for Māori education, *Ka Hikitia* (Ministry of Education, 2008), have been introduced to schools around the country. These initiatives are based on extensive research activities, and the demand for the provision of professional development programmes is on the rise. At the centre of these activities appears to be an intention to provide a better understanding of the concepts and strategies that can offer culturally responsive pedagogical approaches on the one hand, and culturally informed professionals that offer authentic services on the other.

Better communication between cultures is an obvious way of enhancing understanding and strengthening relationships between different cultural groups. Clearly, the most promising contexts for promoting intercultural communication are classrooms, schools and other education settings. The metaphor of huakina mai—opening doorways to allow this to happen – must therefore be a priority. Research in the areas of ethnicity and culture has been useful in terms of broadening our understanding of the impact teachers have on students' academic success, behaviour and motivation. Teachers' attitudes and expectations influence classroom climate and shape both *what* is taught and *how* the teaching is orchestrated (Clark & Clarke, 1996; Eisner, 1994; Graybill, 1997; Macfarlane, 2004, 2007). Teachers need to design instruction in literacy learning that builds on what the students already know, form and maintain positive and effective relationships, and develop a nurturing and inclusive environment (Ministry of Education, 2006). Māori learners often have a preference to work in groups; favour a holistic approach to learning that incorporates all four dimensions of the person—wairua (spiritual), hinengaro (intellectual), tinana (physical) and whatumanawa (emotional); prefer face-to-face contact and discussion; and like their learning to be related to real-life tasks (Ministry of Education, 2009). Particular learning approaches are also highly rated by Māori learners, for example, the tuakana–teina relationship, where an older sibling or cousin supports a younger or less able learner, is a traditional part of Māori society, and provides a positive way to support students when learning to read and write (Ministry of Education, 2006).

There is a strong link between the culture of the student and the attitude of the teacher towards that culture. If a teacher lacks any awareness of the culture of a student, it may result in the teacher taking a negative attitude towards the student, and may also result in lower expectations being placed on the student. Conversely, a teacher who is culturally aware of and responsive to the students in his or her care, is better able to be effective as a result of their skill and empathy, regardless of their cultural difference or similarity. Cordula, Baumert, Julius-McElvany and Peschar (2003) have suggested that students' self-belief is the strongest single predictor of whether they will adopt strategies that make learning effective: simply strengthening students' learning techniques is not, in itself, sufficient to improve achievement. Does this suggest that teachers' attitudes, expectations and approaches to classroom management have a significant impact on student self concept, motivation and achievement?

Huakina mai: Listening to culture

In Aotearoa New Zealand, sensitivity to the cultural background of Māori students is seen as especially important for educators to acknowledge. This concept is based on the assumption that teachers who are culturally sensitive will be better able to understand, and therefore respond to, the learning needs of Māori students - as members of classrooms. Recent research on teachers who are successful when working with Māori students has illuminated a range of concepts and strategies that (when implemented) are also highly beneficial to *all* students who comprise our increasingly diverse classrooms. Specifically, this relates to teachers being willing and able to "connect" with Māori students: who they are and how this may influence the ways they think, feel and act. This is achieved by ensuring that the essence of who the students are as Māori is reflected in both the classroom context (climate, protocols and interactions) and the classroom content (curriculum, teaching and learning). Such teachers are therefore cognisant of utilising particular aspects of tikanga Māori (protocols) to guide the management and social norms of the classroom context, as well as constructing learning activities around mātauranga Māori (Māori knowledge) to guide curriculum content.

Given some of the observations made in the research, it would appear that a lack of understanding of a Māori worldview on the part of the dominant New Zealand culture may be one critical reason why many Māori students are underachieving in mainstream education and are often marginalised or excluded from it. In a society that is frequently described as bicultural or multicultural, it is not surprising that underachievement is often "explained away" by pathologising the individual on the basis of perceived cultural (Māori) deficits. However, it is increasingly common for it to be stated that

> ...the style of content of service delivery in such areas as health, social welfare, and education should be constructed so as to take account of the cultural background of the people receiving these services, or that the service should be culturally appropriate. (Morrisey, 1997, p. 93)

It is time, therefore, to "listen to culture".

Meeting the needs of minority culture students, their parents and the communities in which they live must be seen as an overriding priority, and must be seen in terms of equity and best educational practices. Identifying the learning and behavioural needs of minority culture children in a culturally relevant manner must also be at the heart of any educational philosophies and practices. According to Peer and Reid (2000, p. 1):

> It is necessary that culture-fair principles and practices are considered in the identification and assessment processes, in classrooms practices and provision, the curriculum, in the training of teachers, support assistants and psychologists, in the selection and allocation of resources, in policy and in liaison with parents and the wider community.

It is important for New Zealand educational professionals to strive to produce culturally competent teachers, consultants and organisational systems if we are to motivate Māori learners and raise achievement in reading and writing. Cultural competence is defined as a set of congruent attitudes, practices and policies that enable systems, agencies and professionals to work effectively in cross-cultural situations (Cross, Bazron, Dennis, & Isaacs, 1989). A culturally competent system (or programme) and its representatives acknowledge the importance of culture at all levels, incorporating practices that are culturally aware, sensitive, and appropriate.

Studies carried out in New Zealand have provided evidence that New Zealand schools differ enormously in terms of their effectiveness in carrying out educational and socialising functions for their Māori students (see Clarke & Clarke, 1996). As a result, many Māori students experiencing failure or underachievement in literacy learning, and often consequential behavioural difficulties, may not be getting the social and academic skills needed to participate in contemporary New Zealand society. Teachers have a key function in facilitating socialisation within their classrooms. In a review of nine New Zealand studies, Macfarlane (2003) synthesised some key factors of culturally responsive teaching, offering hope to teachers keen to respond to the challenge of working effectively in diverse classrooms and motivating their students to achieve their potential in literacy achievement and learning in general.

Some schools, some teachers and some approaches to teaching can make a significant difference to the quality of student literacy and learning outcomes for Māori students. The directions taken by the Hei Awhina Mātua programme of the Poutama Pounamu Research Centre (Glynn et al., 1997), the Te Kotahitanga Ministry of Education project (Bishop, Berryman, Richardson, & Tiakiwai, 2002), the South Auckland AIMHI project coordinated by Hill and Hawk (2000), and the Glynn and McNaughton (2002) study are all examples of how behaviour and learning are significantly linked. These studies included connectedness, academic engagement, a supportive environment and recognition of difference as key qualities that make teaching and learning more meaningful for Māori students and students of other ethnic minorities. It is to a study of an exceptional teacher in a New Zealand primary school that this chapter now turns.

Huakina mai: Opening doorways for Māori children in a New Zealand classroom: A case study in motivating students and raising achievement in their literacy learning

Compared with the volumes of literature on learning enhancement and behaviour modification, only a few studies have systematically examined the relationship between ethnic identity and school performance. A study by Macfarlane (2003) reported on a model of good practice that found a positive relationship between ethnic identity—a sense of belonging in Māoritanga— and school performance, through the teacher's ability to stress pride and commitment to the cultural background of all children in the classroom. The study also examined the verbal and non-verbal communication processes between the teacher and students in the classroom.

The classroom, the Paerangi Enrichment Class, had a special function. It was a Māori-controlled Māori-targetted initiative, with an emphasis on improving the literacy and numeracy of the junior school students it served. The study specifically focused on the direct and indirect messages that the teacher, Hera Andrews,[1] communicated to the students, both consciously and subconsciously. Andrews's professional integrity, and the influences this had on students' learning processes,

---

1 A pseudonym.

was explored by employing a range of methods. These included: observation of classroom activities and procedures; focused interviews in groups, and individually with key stakeholders; samples of children's work and analyses of children's progress; and consideration of how successful the programme had been in meeting the outcomes the project had set out to achieve. What emerged were fine examples of culturally relevant teaching—the kind of teaching that calls on the cultural reality of the educational environment to help students to achieve success.

In essence, Andrews was able to instil (or re-instil) in the students a strong self-belief—a sense of self-confidence in their own ability to learn and achieve at school. She believed that all students have potential, strengths and abilities. Andrews therefore had high expectations of the students, while simultaneously ensuring they were able to experience ongoing success in their learning. One of Andrews's skills was to personalise the learning of each of her students so that they were not rated against each other or assessed against some form of whole-class "norm". She ensured that each student set their own targets for learning and reflected on their own gains. And to ensure that the notion of group (co-constructed and supported) learning could continue simultaneously, the classroom culture continually espoused the expectation of shared responsibility for everyone's learning. It was therefore expected that students would go to each other for help and provide assistance wherever possible. The concepts of mana (respect) and ako (reciprocity) were fundamental to Andrews's style of culturally relevant teaching.

The specific student learning outcomes and achievements demonstrated the programme's effectiveness. Testing was carried out at regular intervals to monitor student learning and achievement in Andrews's class. The individual results achieved by the students reinforced the effectiveness of both the programme content and the programme delivery in motivating literacy learning. Further synthesis of these data highlight the overall success of the unit and the progress made in wider terms. After four months in the Paerangi Enrichment Class:
- 60 percent of the Year 2 students achieved oral language gains of more than one year, with the average being 12 months, and a range of 0 to 1 year 7 months
- the average instructional reading improvement was 5.4 Reading Recovery levels (range 0 to 12 levels)

- the average improvement for letter identification was 14 letters/sounds (range 0 to 35)
- the average gain for written vocabulary was 12 words (range 7 to 25 words)
- the average score on the BURT word recognition test was 18 words (range 3 to 32 words).

This overall progress in literacy was achieved with students whose entry data started as low as 3 years 6 months in Assessment of Oral Language, and a score of zero on 50 percent of all tests, after being at school for approximately 10 to 20 months. The students in this cohort had been in the unit for either one or two terms. It is argued that a key characteristic of programmes that attend successfully to Māori students' achievement, such as this Enrichment Class, is cultural responsiveness. This is not to stipulate that teachers be of the same culture as that of the students in order to be effective. What matters is their ability to connect culturally and to promote a cultural presence in their respective learning environments.

Implications for practice

Māori students appreciate learning in an environment where they are able to live as Māori and that acknowledges their spiritual, physical and emotional needs (Ministry of Education, 2009). This culturally supportive environment influences their motivation in literacy learning.

The term "educultural" is used when referring to five concepts that are likely to have an effect on students' literacy learning and teachers' teaching: whanaungatanga (relationships), manaakitanga (empathy), rangatiratanga (leadership), kotahitanga (togetherness) and pūmanawatanga (ambience). These concepts should not be seen in isolation, because they vary together in patterned ways. They are the bases from which teaching strategies and techniques evolve (Macfarlane, 2004).

Acknowledging these concepts and employing a culturally relevant pedagogy will signal to students that their culture matters. Such an approach offers students a dose of what is familiar, in terms of their Māoritanga (Māori heritage) and their Pākehātanga (European heritage). If the learning and teaching connect with the cultures represented in the classroom, then the students are more likely to "switch on". That is how critical the role of the teacher is. That is how critical it is for teachers to develop skills in intercultural communication.

Today's world is characterised by an ever-increasing number of contacts, resulting in communication between people from different ethnic and linguistic backgrounds—communication taking place because of contacts within the areas of commerce, science, media, travel and education. In all of these contexts, successful communication requires an opening of doorways that is constructive and reasoned. Intercultural communication, while not a new phenomenon, may well hold the key to the building of more harmonious relationships for young and old. However, for rangatahi (young people), school is the domain within which intercultural communication is most likely to be facilitated, and this can be summed up in two words: good teaching.

References

Bishop, R., Berryman, M., Richardson, C., & Tiakiwai, S. (2002). *Te Kotahitanga: The experiences of Year 9 and Year 10 Māori students in mainstream classrooms.* A research report to the Ministry of Education. Hamilton: University of Waikato.

Clark, H., & Clarke, R. (1996). Research on the wraparound process and individualised services for children with multiple-system needs. *Journal of Child and Family Studies, 5,* 1–5.

Cordula, A., Baumert J., Julius-McElvany, N., & Peschar, J. (2003). *Learners for life: Students' approaches to learning: Results from PISA 2000.* Paris, France: OECD. Retrieved from http://www.pisa.oecd.org.

Cross, T. L., Bazron, B. J., Dennis, K. W., & Isaacs, M. R. (1989). *Towards a culturally competent system of care, Volume 1.* Washington, DC: National Technical Assistance Centre for Children's Mental Health, Georgetown University Child Development Centre.

Eisner, E. (1994). *The educational imagination: On the design and imagination of school programs* (3rd ed.). New York, NY: Macmillan.

Gillon, G., & Macfarlane, A. (2009, October). *Realising potential in all children.* Keynote address at the Literacy Research Symposium, University of Canterbury, Christchurch.

Glynn, E., Otrel-Cass, K., Cowie, B., & Macfarlane, A. (2008, September). *Culturally responsive pedagogy: Connecting New Zealand teachers of science with their Māori students.*

Paper presented at the European Educational Research Association Annual Conference, Goteborg, Sweden.

Glynn, T., Berryman, M., Bidois, P., Atvars, K., Duffull, T., & Horne, J. (1997). Involving children in research: The Hei Awhina Mātua research project. *Childrenz Issues: Journal of the Children's Issues Centre, 1*(1), 37–43.

Glynn, T., & McNaughton, S. (2002). Trust your own observations: Assessment of reader and tutor behaviour in learning to read English and Māori. *International Journal of Disability, Development and Education, 49*(2), 161-173.

Graybill, S. (1997). Questions of race and culture: How they relate to the classroom for African American students. *Clearing House, 70,* 311–318.

Hill, J., & Hawk, K. (2000). *Making a difference in the classroom: Effective teaching practice in low decile, multicultural schools.* A report prepared for the Ministry of Education and AIMHI Forum. Massey University, Albany: Institute for Professional Development and Educational Research.

Macfarlane, A. (2003). *Culturally inclusive pedagogy for Māori students experiencing learning and behaviour difficulties.* Hamilton: University of Waikato.

Macfarlane, A. (2004). *Kia hiwa rā! Listen to culture: Māori students' plea to educators.* Wellington: NZCER Press.

Macfarlane, A. (2007). *Discipline, democracy and diversity: Working with students with behaviour difficulties.* Wellington: NZCER Press.

Ministry of Education (2006). *Effective literacy practice in Years 5–8.* Wellington: Learning Media.

Ministry of Education (2007). *Education statistics of New Zealand for 2006.* Wellington: Data Management and Analysis Division, Ministry of Education.

Ministry of Education (2008). *Ka Hikitia – Managing for success: Māori Education Strategy 2008–2012* Wellington: Ministry of Education.

Ministry of Education (2009). *Learning foundations for Māori adults: Literacy, language and numeracy research.* Wellington: Ministry of Education.

Morrisey, M. (1997). The uses of culture. *Journal of Intercultural Studies, 18*(2), 93.

Peer, L., & Reid, G. (2000). *Multilingualism, literacy and dyslexia: A challenge for educators.* London: David Fulton Publisher.

CHAPTER 9
Motivating Pasifika students in literacy learning

Jo Fletcher, Faye Parkhill, Amosa Fa'afoi and Tufulasi Taleni

Introduction

This chapter outlines what can motivate upper primary Pasifika students in literacy. These Pasifika students come from a range of different cultural groups, but as minority groups in the New Zealand classroom, these first-, second- or third-generation immigrant Pasifika students encounter similar challenges in learning to read in English, which is often a second language in their home and community. This chapter explores Pasifika students' and parents' perceptions of supports and barriers which may help develop teachers' understanding of ways to promote culturally appropriate pedagogical approaches that support motivation and engagement in learning to read.

Increasing ethnic diversity

The world-wide phenomenon of increasing ethnic diversity in Western countries is shaping the cross-section of populations in today's classrooms. The sociocultural values and beliefs of these diverse learners play an important role, which can influence their motivation to read and their attitude towards reading (Ruddell & Unrau, 2004). This challenges teachers and school leaders to develop and adapt teaching practices and foster stronger home–school partnerships to meet the needs of this more diverse population. To support these changes it is essential that the wider sociopolitical arenas take into account the effect of the power dynamics that mould these shifting cultural and ethnic structures within education and the wider society (de Haan & Elbers, 2005).

Comprehending how educators can achieve this in a positive and effective way is becoming more politically relevant, given that variable school achievement levels (de Haan & Elbers, 2005) among students from different ethnic backgrounds have a generational cyclical effect on educational outcomes and career options. However, it is important to go beyond gross demographic generalisations and take cognisance of "students' lived experiences in family, community and popular culture" that support or inhibit learning (Dooley, 2008, p.117). The concept of cultural capital involves the idea that students' academic achievements are created by the social and cultural resources of families, the community and the school (Bourdieu & Passerson, 1977). Culturally responsive teaching "reflects the values and standards for behaviour of students' home cultures" (Au, 2002, p. 404) and ensures students are taught in a manner that does not negate the cultural capital they bring to their learning. Despite this valid assertion, there are still many students from a range of ethnicities who rely solely on their schooling to gain formal literacy competencies.

Dooley (2008) has reminded us that the social relations in a classroom or school influence students' participation and motivation to learn. Teachers of literacy today are not only challenged by increasingly diverse populations, but also by the continual development of wider interpretations of literacy and innovative text forms made possible through technological advances. Arguably, traditional school literacy learning has privileged a narrow range of approaches that advantage some students but marginalise others (Dooley, 2008). Supporting and motivating students from minority ethnic groups to develop effective reading strategies in English, which is often their second or third language, is a common theme in the literature focusing on the educational needs of migrant and ethnic minority children, an emphasis that is not surprising given the pivotal role of reading in knowledge and skills acquisition (Au, 2002; Kame'enui, Carnine, Dixon, Simmonds, & Coyne, 2002; McNaughton, 2002).

The New Zealand context

Pasifika peoples are one of the two main immigrant ethnic groups in New Zealand. "Pasifika" is a term used to encompass a diverse range of peoples from the South Pacific region now living in New Zealand who have strong family and cultural connections to their Pacific Island countries of origin. The Pasifika population in New Zealand has shown a noticeable increase from 5 percent in 1991 to 6.9 percent in 2006 (Statistics New Zealand, 2007). Samoans make up the largest proportion (49 percent), followed by Cook Island Māori (22 percent), Tongans (19 percent), Niueans (8 percent), Fijians (4 percent), Tokelauans (3 percent) and Tuvaluans (1 percent) (Statistics New Zealand, 2008).

Pasifika children often underachieve in literacy and exhibit disengagement and alienation at school (Alton-Lee, 2003; Chamberlain, 2008; Crooks, Smith, & Flockton, 2009). National and international reports on literacy performance continue to reveal low levels of achievement in reading among Pasifika students (Chamberlain, 2008; Crooks et al., 2009), to the extent that raising the levels of achievement in this area has become a focus for targeted funding in Ministry of Education initiatives (Ministry of Education, 2004, 2007).

Motivating readers

This chapter draws on research undertaken with Pasifika students in their final years of primary schooling (10- to 12-year-olds), an age group in which there has been a much-reported dip or plateauing in reading achievement, both in New Zealand and internationally (see, for example, Brozo, 2005; Farstrup, 2005; Hattie, 2007). Furthermore, in the second cycle of the Progress in International Reading Literacy Study (PIRLS) 2005/06, New Zealand, relative to other higher performing countries, had a notable-sized group of 10-year-old students who were poor readers and who did not reach the PIRLS lower international benchmarks (Chamberlain, 2007). Students in lower socioeconomic schools, Māori (the indigenous people of New Zealand), boys and Pasifika boys and girls were more likely to be in this group of poor readers and to have weaker comprehension scores than other Year 5 students (Chamberlain, 2008).

Students' attitudes to reading are perceived as being part of the wider structure of motivation to read (Sainsbury & Schagen, 2004). When there is decreased motivation to read, this can have a negative impact on reading development. There are specific stages in reading development when this decline can develop (Byrne, 2007). Byrne refers to these as potential "points of discouragement" that can occur during the pathway to reading mastery. Determination to read can be blocked as a child encounters a new process. Learners need to be supported as they negotiate their way through these points of discouragement. For students from minority cultural groups, these potential points of discouragement can be an ongoing lived reality as they grapple not only with different cultural mores and expectations in their school environments, but also often face the challenge of learning, reading and thinking in more than one language (Fa'afoi & Fletcher, 2002).

Learning to read and sustaining motivation to read are critical, yet for all New Zealand children this motivation in reading appears to be declining. The 2008 National Education Monitoring Project (NEMP) for reading assessment for Years 4 and 8 showed that reading as a preferred leisure activity outside of school declined markedly between 2004 and 2008 (Crooks et al., 2009).

When a student has a "positive self-concept as a reader, a desire and tendency to read and a reported enjoyment of or interest in reading" (Sainsbury & Schagen, 2004, p. 374), they are more likely to succeed in their reading. Unfortunately, many students view reading as a school-only activity, often through schools ignoring the power of the students' interests (including culture) as a motivation for reading. They "fail to exploit the experience-to-reading-experience cycle" (Washor, Mojkowski, & Foster, 2009, p. 521). These authors argue that there is a powerful interchange between students' experiences of the world and what they read. This "cycle of experience and reading—a cycle of life to text and text to life—is at the heart of literacy learning" (p. 521). In this context, the New Zealand Ministry of Education (2003, p. 12) advocates that:

> effective practice involves using and creating rich texts. These relate to students' interests, draw on and affirm their social and cultural identities, use authentic language, and motivate and challenge them as learners.

Supporting and motivating Pasifika students

It is critical not to regard immigrant groups as a homogeneous group. Within Pasifika people there are many distinct cultural groups, such as Samoan, Tongan, Tokelauan and Niuean. Each is diverse in cultural practices and language. Ferguson, Gorinski, Wendt Samu and Mara (2008, p. 23), in their literature review on the experiences of Pasifika learners, reiterate that:

> the rich variety of Pasifika backgrounds and the range of learning types amongst Pasifika learners were identified as problematic in the literature because of the inherent challenges they pose in terms of inclusion and potential tokenism.

Adding to this diversity, Pasifika populations comprise recently arrived immigrants and second- or third-generation New Zealand-born Pasifika people, and many have mixed cultural heritages crossing a range of ethnicities.

Culture

For Pasifika learners, the construction of knowledge, and therefore their cultural capital, is not always aligned with the underpinning literacy (and therefore reading) pedagogy that has been derived from eurocentric values. Pasifika children demonstrate a strong desire not only to engage with and succeed in the mainstream culture but also to maintain their own cultural identity, and to see this represented in their texts and other forms of classroom media. In our studies of Pasifika children and parents we used open-ended focus group interviews. The initial questions that we asked guided rather than directed the interview. Our aim was to facilitate a session that did not limit the talk to a predetermined agenda (Rapley, 2007), so allowing for the unexpected and for the reality of the interviewees' contexts to be part of their commentary. In one of our studies, (Fletcher, Parkhill, Fa'afoi & Taleni, 2006) comprising 37 low-achieving Pasifika children, nearly two-thirds articulated a desire to write about their own culture but reported that they seldom had the opportunity to write about the cultural contexts and experiences that were part of their daily lives. These children's stated desire to have more opportunities to write and read about their own culture is reinforced by literature on meeting the needs of diverse students (Alton-Lee, 2003; Bishop & Glynn, 1999; Nieto, 2002; Villegas & Lucas, 2002).

In another study (Parkhill, Fletcher, & Fa'afoi, 2005) of high-achieving Pasifika students there was a strong emphasis on the acceptance and use of the students' home languages in the school environment, a visible use of reading material about Pasifika people, provision by the school of Pasifika costumes for culturally significant occasions and a religious ethos that aligned with the children's cultural beliefs and practices.

Pasifika families, particularly in low-income areas, often have two or more sets of cultures to support: their own culture or cultures, and the culture of the wider New Zealand society, generally represented by the school (Gorinski & Fraser, 2006). The Pasifika values of respect for elders (such as parents, ministers and teachers) and the church, plus the centrality of the Bible and reading it at home and at church, are critical factors that motivate reading.

The Pasifika parents deemed it critical that their children were confident speakers of their first language, such as Samoan or Tongan. One parent explained:

> ... I think the language is a gift of the tongue. It is part of belonging, the heritage and all of that. It's giving something back to our children to be proud of, whether they can speak it fluently or not. It is part of their belonging to that place. (Fletcher, Parkhill, Taleni, Fa'afoi, & O'Regan, 2009, p. 30).

This acknowledgment in schools of a Pasifika student's first language seemed to be influential in building Pasifika students' confidence, on the premise that when Pacific languages are used, the students feel that their teachers really care about their language and culture (Fletcher, et al., 2009). Concurring with this notion, Tuafuti and McCaffery (2005) argue that improving and motivating Pasifika students in their self-esteem, self-discipline and self-identity entails the inclusion of Pasifika language and cultural considerations in all parts of Pasifika students' education.

Reading

The teachers and parents from our research studies (see, for example, Fletcher et al., 2009; Parkhill et al., 2005) perceived that, for Pasifika students, decoding words was a strength but that understanding the meaning of the words and comprehending the text were weaknesses. The comment of one Pasifika mother in this regard was typical:

> When they read the books and then you ask them something, they don't actually understand what they're actually reading. Most Pacific Islanders have problems because they can read [decode] and speak it [but] they don't always understand what they're reading. (Fletcher, et al., 2009, p. 29).

Some words in reading texts were said to relate to things that the Pasifika students had not yet experienced and/or that were unfamiliar concepts, while other words may not be commonly used or have equivalent translations in their different Pasifika first languages.

Barriers and motivators

Teachers selecting and reading aloud to the whole class a book that is interesting and engaging was seen as a critical enabler. The students disliked the use of worksheets after a guided group lesson, preferring to silently read a text of their choice. The practice of reading aloud one by one from their text during guided reading or their own writing was strongly disliked. They often felt embarrassment and humiliation when required to read aloud in class, because it could result in subtle forms of teasing by peers, particularly non-Pasifika students. Excessive classroom noise during literacy instruction was perceived as a barrier to learning to read. Likewise, the students reported that ineffective classroom management distracted them from their learning.

Taking risks

Pasifika students are often reluctant to take risks (Fletcher et al., 2009). In literacy learning this might, for example, include predicting what will come next in the text, which often requires drawing on prior knowledge, experience of the world and knowledge of the text content (Cullen, 2002). It can involve making predictions or inferring meaning quickly and often automatically. When students take risks, both in oral reading and in comprehension, effective teachers encourage this endeavour and acknowledge that they are learning how to unlock and predict increasingly complex text. This action of risk taking is an additional challenge for many Pasifika students, for whom the content of the material may be outside their realm of experiences and compound their fear of making a mistake (Fletcher et al., 2006). A teacher of Pasifika students, like other teachers, explained that the children would rather appear as if they don't respect learning because it's not valuable, than feel they are going to look stupid doing something related to words.

Implications for practice

What needs to be disentangled when looking at the achievement of any one ethnic group, and working out how to accentuate what motivates reading achievement and what can form potential "points of discouragement", is the interplay of variables for that group. We suggest that the classroom and school practices that support and motivate Pasifika students' literacy acquisition include:

- the provision of more culturally inclusive resources, particularly reading texts
- inclusion of Pasifika language, songs and cultural practices
- opportunities for children to read and write about their own culture
- quiet classrooms when children are writing and reading
- not forcing children to read aloud in a reading group or to the whole class
- teachers providing more explicit scaffolds for writing
- teachers developing the ability to actively engage all children when they (the teachers) read aloud
- teachers providing more detailed feedback and feedforward on the children's writing
- effective classroom management
- decreasing and discouraging instances of bullying, both inside and outside the classroom (Fletcher, Parkhill, & Fa'afoi, 2005).

A reader and literacy learner acquires sociocultural values and beliefs through their family, peer groups and community interaction, which profoundly influence their reading development and success in literacy learning (Ruddell & Unrau, 2004). In a similar vein, Pasifika students are motivated to learn when their sociocultural values and beliefs align with, or are acknowledged, valued and respected by, those of their teacher and the wider school.

References

Alton-Lee, A. (2003). *Quality teaching for diverse students in schooling: Best evidence synthesis*. Wellington: Ministry of Education.

Au, K. (2002). Multicultural factors and the effect of the instruction of students of diverse backgrounds. In A. E. Farstrup & S. J. Samuels (Eds.), *What research has to say about reading* (pp. 392–414). Newark, DE: International Reading Association.

Biddulph, F., Biddulph, J., & Biddulph, C. (2003). *The complexity of community and family influences on children's achievement in New Zealand: Best evidence synthesis*. Wellington: Ministry of Education.

Bourdieu, P., & Passerson, J. C. (1977). *Reproduction in education, society and culture*. London: Sage.

Brozo, W. (2005). Avoiding the "fourth-grade slump". *Thinking Classroom, 6*(4), 48.

Byrne, B. (2007). Theories of learning to read. In M. J. Snowling & C. Hulme (Eds.), *The science of reading: A handbook* (pp. 104–119). Malden, MA: Blackwell.

Chamberlain, M. (2007). *Reading literacy in New Zealand: An overview of New Zealand's results from the Progress in International Reading Literacy Study (PIRLS) 2005/2006*. Retrieved 21 September 2009, from http://www.educationcounts.govt.nz/publications/series/2539/pirls_0506/16390

Chamberlain, M. (2008). *PIRLS 2005/2006 in New Zealand: An overview of national findings from the second cycle of the Progress in International Reading Literacy Study (PIRLS)*. Retrieved 6 January 2009, from http://www.educationcounts.govt.nz/publications/series/2539/pirls_0506/34905/34905/7

Crooks, T., Smith, J., & Flockton, L. (2009). *National Education Monitoring Project: Reading and speaking assessment results for 2008*. Dunedin: Educational Assessment Research Unit, University of Otago.

Cullen, J. (2002). The social and cultural contexts of early literacy: Making the links between homes, centres and schools. In P. Adams & H. Ryan (Eds.), *Learning to read in Aotearoa New Zealand: A collaboration between early childhood educators, families and schools*. Palmerston North: Dunmore Press.

de Haan, M., & Elbers, E. (2005). Peer tutoring in a multiethnic classroom in the Netherlands: A multiperspective analysis of diversity. *Comparative Education Review, 49*(3), 365–388.

Dooley, K. (2008). Multiliteracies and pedagogies of new learning for students of English as a second language. In A. Healy (Ed.), *Multiliteracies and diversity in education* (pp. 102–125). South Melbourne: Oxford University Press.

Fa'afoi, A., & Fletcher, J. (2002). Na hakahita ki tagata Pahefika i te akoga haka haiakoga: Identifying barriers for Pacific Islands student teachers *Many Voices, 19*, 24–31.

Farstrup, A. E. (2005). Qualified reading specialists: More important than ever. *Reading Today, 23*(3), 18.

Ferguson, P. B., Gorinski, R., Wendt Samu, T., & Mara, D. (2008). *Literature review on the experience of Pasifika learners in the classroom.* Wellington: Ministry of Education.

Fletcher, J., Parkhill, F., & Fa'afoi, A. (2005). What factors promote and support Pasifika students in reading and writing? set: *Research Information for Teachers, 2*, 2–8.

Fletcher, J., Parkhill, F., Fa'afoi, & Taleni, T. (2006). Pasifika students' perceptions of barriers and support to reading and writing achievement in New Zealand schools. *New Zealand Journal of Educational Studies, 4*(2), 163–182.

Fletcher, J., Parkhill, F., Taleni, T., Fa'afoi, A., & O'Regan, B. (2009). Pasifika students: Teachers and parents voice their perceptions of what impacts on Pasifika students' achievement in literacy, language and learning. *Teaching and Teacher Education, 25*, 24–33.

Gorinski, R., & Fraser, C. (2006). *Literature review on the effective engagement of Pasifika parents and communities in education.* Wellington: Ministry of Education.

Hattie, J. (2007). The status of reading in New Zealand schools: The upper primary plateau problem (UP). *Reading Forum NZ, 22*(3), 25–39.

Kame'enui, E. J., Carnine, D. W., Dixon, R. C., Simmonds, D. C., & Coyne, M. D. (2002). *Effective teaching strategies that accommodate diverse learners* (2nd ed.). Upper Saddle River, NJ: Merrill Prentice Hall.

McNaughton, S. (2002). *Meeting of minds.* Wellington: Learning Media.

Ministry of Education. (2004). *Focus on Pasifika achievement in reading literacy.* Retrieved from http://www.minedu.govt.nz

Ministry of Education. (2007). *Pasifika Education Plan.* Wellington: Author.

Parkhill, F., Fletcher, J., & Fa'afoi, A. (2005). What makes for success?: Current literacy practices and the impact of family and community on Pasifika students' literacy learning. *New Zealand Journal of Educational Studies, 40*(1&2), 61–84.

Rapley, T. (2007). Interviews. In C. Seale, G. Gobo, J. Gubrium, & D. Silverman (Eds.), *Qualititive Research Practice* (pp. 15–33). Los Angeles: Sage.

Ruddell, R., & Unrau, N. (2004). Reading as a meaning-construction process: The reader, the text, and the teacher. In R. Ruddell & N. Unrau (Eds.), *Theoretical models and processes of reading* (5th ed., pp. 1462–1521). Newark, DE: International Reading Association.

Sainsbury, M., & Schagen, I. (2004). Attitudes to reading at ages nine and eleven. *Journal of Research in Reading, 27*(4), 373–386.

Statistics New Zealand. (2008). *Pacific profiles: 2006*. Retrieved 23 May 2008, from http://www.stats.govt.nz/analytical-reports/pacific-profiles-2006/default.htm

Washor, E., Mojkowski, C., & Foster, D. (2009). Living literacy: A cycle of life to text and text to life. *Phi Delta Kappan, 90*(7) 521–523.

CHAPTER 10

Asian student voices: Approaches in reading that motivate or provoke dissonance in their journey towards being successful readers of English

Faye Parkhill and Jo Fletcher

Introduction

This chapter focuses on Asian students in their final years of primary schooling and what they perceived as having motivated their literacy learning. Alverman (2002) has argued that the degree of student engagement can be a mediating factor through which classroom literacy practices can influence student achievement. Many authors have contended that home–school connections, cultural responsiveness in classroom programmes and recognising children's home languages can assist in the enhancement of literacy learning for the growing number of Asian students in English-speaking classrooms (Kong & Pearson, 2003; Lily, 2001; Palmer, Chen, Chang, & Lechere, 2006).

Between 2001 and 2006 the number of Asians in the New Zealand population increased almost 50 percent, from 238,176 people in 2001 to 354,552 people in 2006. This was the fastest rate of increase for any ethnic group within New Zealand. Within this Asian category, the two fastest-growing groups have been Chinese and Korean, with the former experiencing a 40.5 percent rate of increase between 2001 and 2006 and the latter a 61.8 percent rate of increase over the same period (Statistics New Zealand, 2007). This influx of Asian immigrants to New Zealand has altered the ratio of other ethnic groups, with the Asian ethnic groups having now superseded the combined Pasifika groups and they are fast catching up to Māori. The Asian population is projected to increase from 400,000 in 2006 to 790,000 in 2026 (Statistics New Zealand, 2008). A focus on this ethnicity regarding the appropriateness of current literacy pedagogy to meet their learning needs in New Zealand schools is therefore now both pertinent and well justified.

Literacy achievement

In contrast to Māori and Pasifika people, the Asian population overall is achieving well in literacy in the European-dominated society of New Zealand. For example, in the Progress in International Reading Literacy Study (PIRLS) of 2005/06, conducted by the International Association for the Evaluation of Educational Achievement (IEA), the summary of student achievement for Year 5 New Zealand students cited mean achievement scores for European (552) and Asian (550) students that were significantly higher than the international mean (500), while the mean scores for Māori (448) and Pasifika (479) students were significantly lower than the international mean (Ministry of Education, 2009). European and Asian students also tended to be more positive towards reading and had a higher self-concept than Māori and Pasifika students. Moreover, Asian students were more positive in 2005/06 than in the previous PIRLS survey in 2001.

Previous evidence of literacy achievement in the Programme for International Student Assessment (PISA), carried out in 2000 and involving nearly 3,700 New Zealand 15-year-olds, showed a clear link between the performance of students and their expressed engagement, level of interest and positive attitudes towards school (Ministry of Education, 2002). The Asian students, when compared to the other ethnic groups within the country, indicated a stronger interest in reading, reported the highest level of engagement in reading and reported the widest range of reading material. PISA also identified that the effective learners in the study used a range of learning strategies. Of this group of learners, Asian students made more use than other ethnic groups of control strategies, such as deciding what they needed to learn, checking back on what they had learnt and figuring out what strategies they had not really understood. They made more use of memorisation strategies and reported the most frequent use of elaboration strategies, such as relating new material to what they already knew and deciding how what they had learnt could be used in the real world. Generally speaking, the evidence suggests that Asian students in New Zealand have strong learning dispositions: those who participated in PISA also reported working more competitively and investing more time than any other ethnic group in their homework. Their self-concept of their ability in English was relatively low, but there was some indication that they might have been underestimating their ability in English.

In New Zealand, Asian students represent a diversity of cultural and linguistic identities, such as South Korean, Chinese, Malaysian and Taiwanese, and educators need to acknowledge the risks in treating Asian students as a homogeneous group. Motivational beliefs act as a frame of reference that influences students' thinking, feelings and actions towards learning. Engaged students are motivated by the material presented, are able to use a range of strategies to ensure comprehension, and construct new knowledge as a result of interactions with text, usually through a socially interactive learning context (King, 2002).

For Asian students (and, in fact, for all students), literacy practices in the classroom can help or hinder the development of intrinsic motivation, which helps to ensure they reach their potential as literacy learners. Guthrie and Wigfield (2000) reported that different instructional practices may not in themselves influence students' outcomes. They identified four factors in their model for student engagement: the fostering of student motivation, which includes self-efficacy and goal setting; strategic use of literacy processes; growth in conceptual knowledge, such as knowledge of texts and information-processing strategies; and social interaction.

Approaches in literacy learning that provoke dissonance

For teachers to better understand how to motivate Asian students, they may benefit from knowing what demotivates their literacy learning. For example, although

the Asian students in a study completed by the authors (Fletcher & Parkhill, 2007) were achieving at or above the average in reading in standardised tests, they still identified five barriers affecting motivation in learning to read in English:
- individually reading aloud in guided reading groups
- reading their own writing aloud to the class and/or a passage of text by another author
- hearing the teacher read aloud an inappropriate choice of text and/or with a lack of expression
- completing written comprehension questions and worksheets after a guided reading lesson
- engaging in buddy reading.

Although these barriers refer directly to instructional practices, it was the teachers' interpretation and implementation of approaches, such as guided reading or buddy reading, that were identified as points of discouragement.

These five practices are reportedly still widely implemented in New Zealand class programmes despite some caution about their inappropriateness in the professional literature (Ministry of Education, 2003, 2006). Students said that they did not like, and had not in previous years liked, reading aloud in guided reading sessions. The students made comments such as that reading aloud leads to other students becoming unfocused, students have an aversion to being singled out and students ostracise those reading, particularly if they make a mistake. Similarly, reading aloud to the whole class was out of favour with the majority of the students.

When teachers read aloud, the students emphasised that the teacher needs to inject expression and voice characterisation to make the story come alive. Teachers need to have oral reading skills that capture the changing tenor and mood within the story line and make the characters come to life within the story. This finding suggests that if the teacher reading aloud is to have positive impact, they must select appropriate texts that engage children by relating to their world experiences, and that frequently challenge them to think about others, like themselves, who are confronting similar or different relationships and issues. Along with this approach, teachers need to have oral reading skills that capture the changing tenor and mood within the storyline and make the characters come to life within the story.

Written comprehension questions and/or worksheets as a follow-up activity after guided reading were viewed as another demotivating practice. This corresponds to Allington's (2001) argument that much teaching for comprehension involves useless activities, such as worksheets with comprehension questions, graphic organisers or hidden word searches. The students' comments indicated that they found the worksheets did not promote enjoyment of and understanding in reading. When we asked the participating children to state the best thing they could do when the teacher took another reading group, the students collectively said that it was personal reading.

Approaches to literacy learning that motivate Asian students

The Asian students were informative about options, other than worksheets, they could do after guided reading. The most popular of these were ones that involved developing their own activities. Foremost among these was creating their own questions in relation to the text, because it held their interest and so helped them gain deeper understanding of the text. This is similar to inquiry learning, where students develop their own questions. This approach positions students as dynamically involved in learning and continually restructuring understanding. It requires students to be active learners, which means they can develop skills and attitudes that enable them to seek resolutions to questions, and from there to construct new knowledge (Hanlon, 2004). Other preferred activities for the students included summarising the story or book, engaging in reading games, writing their own descriptions of the text and practising and performing plays related to the texts.

In a study by Kong and Pearson (2003) of literacy practices for linguistically diverse learners, five features of classroom practice were identified that helped to create and support learning. In many respects these findings reflected the Asian students' responses described here in terms of what is considered to be effective literacy practice for all learners (Ministry of Education, 2003, 2006):
- There was recognition by the teacher of the rich experiences that students bring to school.
- There were opportunities to engage in shared responses to quality literature.

- Students were encouraged to think critically through the use of high-level questioning.
- The teachers used explicit and deliberate acts of teaching (Ministry of Education, 2003, 2006) and also assumed the role of a learner.
- The teachers maintained high expectations, and the students were challenged in their learning.

Parental influences affecting literacy learning

The students' comments indicated that they did not see reading about their own cultures as an activity that would support their literacy learning. The students discussed the influence of their parents on their reading ability and identified them as having an important role in supporting their reading achievement. They described their parents as being organised and efficient in ensuring that they (the students) had opportunities to read and access to interesting books, both in the home and by regularly getting books from the local library. In their analyses of IEA reading literacy studies, Yang-Hansen, Rosén, and Gustafsson (2007) reported that the number of books in the home is a strong predictor of reading achievement across all societies, in part because, as these researchers explained, this variable is an indicator of socioeconomic status.

Chiu and Ko (2007), in their analysis of data from the field test in Taiwan for PIRLS 2006, noted a significant link between parental reading attitudes and children's positive reading behaviours. Parents who had positive attitudes to reading and provided a rich environment and resources fostered children's reading abilities. The authors also observed that Chinese educational thought has a Confucian influence, which places considerable emphasis on personal responsibility for one's own learning, and considers children to be obligated to their parents to achieve to their highest possible level (see also Reagan, 2000). Dyson (2001) has argued that Asian parents tend to have high expectations for their children to succeed academically, which also includes the development of critical thinking, practical skills and behavioural discipline.

In our study, also evident was the students' respect for their parents, many of whom were continuing their education by improving their use of or learning of

English. Many students revealed that they could speak English better than their parents and that they often helped their parents with both spoken and written English. Li (2004, cited in Kennedy & Trong, 2007) has suggested that Asian people tend to view education as a lifetime pursuit that aligns with one's moral and social status, whereas Western culture links education with the achievement of a personal goal (see also Myrberg & Rosén, 2007, in this regard). Furthermore, the overall home backgrounds of the students in a class or school influence student motivation, aspirations and achievement (Elijio, 2007). Reading literacy, the focus for this investigation, is central to success across all curriculum areas, and supportive home environments of the kind described above usually engage in and encourage children's reading, which leads to more frequent independent reading, and that reading mileage in return can improve reading achievement.

These influences may also have been compounded by the fact that many of the children who participated in the research were receiving after-school tuition, a practice common in many Asian countries (see, for example, Xu & Lewis, 2002). Li (2003) has emphasised the importance attached to becoming literate in English by Asian immigrants, while Ning (2007), when discussing English teaching in China, states that learning English is highly regarded and is a compulsory subject from Grade 3.

The Asian students in our study did not find culturally aligned resources and learning contexts to be paramount, which conflicts somewhat with the findings of many studies on Asian students (see, for example, Dyson, 2001, and others; Lily, 2001; Palmer et al., 2006). This was surprising, particularly as these students said that the culture and resources of the schools supported their learning. Their comments suggested that they were not interested in reading about their own cultures. Rather, they indicated an enthusiasm to read stories and articles set in the New Zealand context. Only one expressed an interest in following up on his culture when he spoke of reading, but even here it was in terms of writing a biography about a prominent Asian person rather than an interest in his culture per se. King (2002) has argued that engaged readers are those who are motivated by the texts in a variety of forms, including multimodal text types. She also contends that the construction of new knowledge from interaction with texts, along with social interaction with peers, motivates literacy learners. The responses of the Asian students in our study supported these pedagogical underpinnings.

Conclusion

When looking at how to motivate Asian students, teachers and the wider school community should consider how to provide a supportive learning environment that acknowledges the intrinsic role that positive home–school connections play in fostering learning. Asian students tend to have a very strong allegiance to their parents and wider family. The views and opinions of these family members are influential in their learning, and in order to best capitalise on this teachers and educational leaders should forge strong links so that there is a shared understanding of goals and aspirations. Countering the barrier of language, particularly with many Asian parents who have limited English, requires schools to think about how they can help overcome this barrier within their school situation.

Implications for practice

Here are some suggestions for your practice in the classroom:
- Vary activities, and, where possible, allow for student choice in what they read after instructional reading and the types of independent reading activities they can engage in.
- Develop your skill in reading aloud and seek the opinions of Asian students in your choice of texts.
- Capitalise on parental interest and involvement.
- Realise that some Asian students prefer a wide range of texts, which may not necessarily be related to their culture.

References

Allington, R. L. (2001). *What really matters for struggling readers: Designing research-based programs*. New York: Addison-Wesley Educational.

Alverman, D. (2002). Effective literacy instruction for adolescents. *Journal of Literacy Research*, 34(2), 189–208.

Chiu, C. -H., & Ko, H. -W. (2007). Relationships between parental factors and children's reading behaviors and attitudes: Results from the PIRLS 2005 field test in Taiwan. In *The second IEA research conference: Proceedings of the IEA IRC-2006* (vol. 2, pp. 249–260). Amsterdam: International Association for the Evaluation of Educational Achievement.

Dyson, L. (2001). Home–school communication and expectations of recent Chinese immigrants. *Canadian Journal of Education, 26*(3), 455–470.

Elijio, A. (2007). Reading achievements in urban and rural communities: A comparative analysis of equity in education. In *The second IEA research conference: Proceedings of the IEA IRC-2006* (vol. 2, pp. 169–176). Amsterdam: International Association for the Evaluation of Educational Achievement.

Guthrie, J. T., & Wigfield, A. (2000). Engagement and motivation in reading. In M. K. Kamil, P. B. Mosenthal, P. D. Pearson, & R. Barr (Eds.), *Handbook of reading research* (pp. 403–422). Mahwah, NJ: Erlbaum.

Hanlon, D. (2004). Beyond the curriculum wars—understanding. *Curriculum Perspectives, 24*(1), 55–57.

Kennedy, A., & Trong, K. (2007). A comparison of fourth-graders' academic self-concept and attitudes toward reading, mathematics, and science in PIRLS and TIMSS countries. In *The second IEA research conference: Proceedings of the IEA IRC-2006* (vol. 2, pp. 49–60). Amsterdam: International Association for the Evaluation of Educational Achievement.

King, J. (2002). Using DVD feature films in the EFL classroom. *Computer Assisted Language Learning, 15*(5), 509–523.

Kong, A., & Pearson, P. D. (2003). The road to participation: The construction of a literacy practice in a learning community of linguistically diverse learners. *Research in the Teaching of English, 38*(1), 85–124.

Li, G. (2003). Literacy, culture, and politics of schooling: Counter-narratives of a Chinese Canadian family. *Anthropology and Education Quarterly, 34*(2), 182–195. Retrieved 6 August 2007, from

http://proquest.umi.com.ezproxy.canterbury.ac.nz/pqdweb?did=353646431&sid=3&Fmt=4&clientid=13346&rqt=309andVName=PQD

Ministry of Education. (2002). *PISA 2000: Overview of selected New Zealand findings*. Retrieved 7 August 2007, from

http://educationcounts.edcentre.govt.nz/publications/downloads/pisa.overview.2000.pdf

Ministry of Education. (2003). *Effective literacy practice in years 1–4*. Wellington: Learning Media.

Ministry of Education. (2006). *Effective literacy practice in years 5–8*. Wellington: Learning Media.

Ministry of Education. (2009). *Annual report: Part one: Participation, engagement and achievement*. Retrieved 12 April 2010, from

http://www.minedu.govt.nz/theMinistry/PublicationsAndResources/AnnualReport/AnnualReport09/PartOne/ParticipationEngagementAchievement.aspx

Myrberg, E., & Rosén, M. (2007). A cross-country comparison of direct and indirect effects of parents' level of education on students' reading achievement. In *The second IEA research conference: Proceedings of the IEA IRC-2006* (vol. 2, pp. 307–318). Amsterdam: International Association for the Evaluation of Educational Achievement.

Ning, H. (2007, September). *Using co-operative learning in EFL teaching with tertiary students in China*. Paper presented at a research seminar, University of Canterbury, Christchurch.

Palmer, B. C., Chen, C. I., Chang, S., & Lechere, J. T. (2006). The impact of biculturalism on language and literacy development: Teaching Chinese English language learners. *Reading Horizons, 46*(4), 239–265.

Reagan, T. (2000). *Non-Western educational traditions*. London: Erlbaum.

Statistics New Zealand. (2007). *Profile of New Zealander responses, ethnicity question: 2006 Census*. Retrieved 12 April 2010, from

http://search.stats.govt.nz/search?p=KK&srid=S2%2d1&lbc=statsnz&ts=custom&pw=2006%20census%20ethnicity&uid=548274463&isort=score&w=ethnicity%202006&rk=

Statistics New Zealand. (2008). *National ethnic population projections: 2006 (base)—2026*. Retrieved 12 April 2010, from

http://search.stats.govt.nz/search?w=Ethnicity&af=ctype%3Astatistics+ctype%3Ainfoaboutstats

Xu, S., & Lewis, M. (2002). Innovation in a Chinese English-language school. *Many Voices, 19*, 12–13.

Yang-Hansen, K., Rosén, M., & Gustafsson, J. E. (2007). *Effects of socio-economic status on reading achievement at collective and individual levels in Sweden in 1991 and 2001*. Retrieved 20 September 2007, from http://www.iea.nl/irc2004-pirls.html

CHAPTER 11
Playing with text

Janinka Greenwood

Introduction

A class of six-year-olds are writing a letter to the police. They are in collective role as members of the Bear family, whose house has been vandalised by Goldilocks. The teacher takes their dictation on the whiteboard. She writes exactly what they suggest, but at times she intervenes with questions, such as "Will they understand what we mean here?" or "Do they need more detail?" When the letter is finished, the teacher checks: "Have we got it right?", "Is there anything we want to change?" When the class are satisfied with their letter, the teacher picks up the narrative: "And so when this letter arrived at the police station the officer rang up the Bear household", and, inviting someone in the class to pick up the phone, she takes the role of police officer, and the next frame of the drama unfolds.

The drama is part of the class's literacy programme, and the teacher uses the various frames to engage and motivate students, to contextualise their learning tasks and to facilitate an inclusive and multilevel approach to reading, writing and other facets of sociocultural literacy.

This chapter explores ways in which the creative and interactive processes of drama can be used to contextualise and animate text (of various kinds) and thereby motivate learners. I examine how a number of characteristics of drama processes—namely, *agency*, the use of *role* and *framing*, *deconstructive strategies* and *performance*—can be actively manipulated to increase motivation in reading and to engage learners in negotiating the relationship between text and meaning. I illustrate these concepts by reference to two applied dramas designed to engage students in particular aspects of literacy.

First, however, I briefly examine the relationship between motivation and learning in literacy. I discuss the complexity of skills and attitudes involved in literacy, the importance of learning dispositions as well as competencies and the relationship between motivation and meaning making.

Connections between literacy and motivation

Reading and writing are complex activities: they involve not only the graphophonic decoding and encoding of text and the comprehension and manipulation of words and grammatical structures (Ehri, 2006; Pressley, 2006), but also the making of personal and social meaning (DeZutter, 2007; Gee, 2000). And in fact literacy involves more than reading and writing; it also involves making meaning from and through a range of communicative codes that today involve using technologies such as the Internet, emailing and texting (Healy, 2008).

Learning involves the development of both competencies and disposition. Carr and Claxton (2004) argue that competencies are necessary but not sufficient. Children (along with older learners) need to be disposed to learn and willing to take learning opportunities. In their words, "education for lifelong learning has to attend to the cultivating of a positive learning disposition as well as of effective learning skills" (p. 106). Although the development of a positive learning disposition is individual, and to some extent independent of the competencies taught by a teacher, the direction it takes is to a large extent shaped by experience, in terms of both personal engagement in particular activities and the values and aspirations acquired from the wider sociocultural context.

Although motivation is a complex—and sometimes contested—construct (Schunk, Pintrich, & Meece, 2008), for the purposes of this discussion the term "motivation" is used to denote the process that gets students going, makes tasks personally meaningful and helps students to complete tasks.

The role of drama

There is already a significant body of writing on the role that process drama can play in developing literacy. The use of drama to contextualise, deconstruct, emotionally engage with and critically reflect on literature, with students of all ages, has been widely discussed, notably by Heathcote and Bolton (1995); Millar and Saxton (2004); and O'Toole and Dunn (2002); Wagner (1998) relates the fictional frames, emotional engagement and physicality of process drama to Gardner's multiple intelligences (Gardner, 1993) and examines how the careful manipulation of a process drama may not only provide a way to connect with the diverse learning styles and types of intelligence within a class, but may also be targeted to address specific reading or writing tasks. For example, recent work by Greenwood and Sæbo (2009) reports how process drama motivates students in second-language learning and provides a context in which they feel safe to experiment with vocabulary and sentence structures, and can play with the target language beyond the limitations offered in textbook exercises.

Much of the literature conveys an excitement about the efficacy of drama as a tool for various kinds of learning, but also an understanding that drama in itself is not a magic wand: that what it offers are specific strategies and processes that need to be skilfully manipulated by a teacher to create opportunities for learning. This chapter examines five of the "tools of trade" that I consider particularly useful for contextualising and animating text and thereby motivating learners.

The first of these is *agency*. Drama—particularly in the forms of improvisation, process drama and devising—invites participants to *act*: to take responsibility for making something, and to invest what they make with an imprint of their choice. This contrasts with the passivity that occurs in those classrooms where students see schooling as a process of simply following the teacher's instructions or returning the answers they think the teacher expects.

The second tool is the exploration and management of *role*. Role allows participants to be other than the way they have constructed themselves to be, or have been constructed to be, in real life. It may allow them to explore someone else's situation, or to play with and chance some aspect of their own situation. It also allows a certain personal safety during exploration, because it is not the individual who says or does something: it is the role.

The third tool is the use of *framing*. Drama allows a range of strategies for framing action. One is the use of fictional contexts. Another is the use of conventions of enactment, such as freeze frame or voices in the head. Such strategies allow quite intense emotions, problems or conflicts to be explored within a frame that allows intensity at the same time as it holds them separate from the real life of the participants.

The fourth tool is a palette of processes for *analysis and deconstruction*. The manipulation of frames in drama may challenge participants to tease out the text and subtext to develop back story, to see events from another point of view, to envisage different outcomes or to synthesise ideas and represent them in symbolic form.

The fifth tool is *performance*, or, to play a little with the word, pre-form-ance. In the process of building up to performance (public and planned, or spontaneous within a process drama), participants rehearse: they try out, refine and develop a satisfying fit. In performance itself they have the opportunity to make a mark, physically and before witnesses. In some cases the performance can become a process of pre-forming the expertise they expect to gain later in their lives: trialling and claiming future roles.

The next pages illustrate through two dramas, *Goldilocks in Trouble* and *Mallory House*, how these clusters of strategies might work in action. The dramas and concepts in this discussion have grown out of practitioner research (mine and others, some of which is cited above). My focus here, however, is not on reporting the detail of that research but rather in showing how teachers can use the work to motivate and focus their students. And because it is drama that is being discussed, the examples are offered as part of the unfolding of a dramatic narrative.

Goldilocks in Trouble

Goldilocks in Trouble (Greenwood, 2005) is a drama I have played around with and adapted for various groups of students in New Zealand and internationally. (Process dramas can be compared to commedia dell'arte: they are passed on through practice, and they have a basic concept and form, and repertoire of possibilities, that are adapted and refined to meet the needs of the audience and situation.) The action starts where the traditional story finishes: the Bears find the havoc in their house and report it to the police, and the police challenge Goldilocks's family to take responsibility for ensuring that Goldilocks answers for her actions.

The work might start with the teacher saying something like, "Once there was this little girl. Oh, I've forgotten her name! It was . . . maybe you can remember . . . she had this yellow hair …" Sooner rather than later the students will prompt, "Goldilocks!" "That's right!" says the surprised teacher, and asks to be reminded of the story. (If the class is one that does not know the story, the teacher can seed familiarity with an earlier reading.) "And if we were to make a comic strip of the story," the teacher could prompt, "say, six frames, what might they look like?" Together the teacher and the students select the key moments of the story, with each one allocated to a group, the members of which prepare a freeze frame. The frames are presented in sequence.

Two parallel drama strategies are being employed here. First, the teacher is taking the role of someone who is not very sure about the story, and in doing so is endowing her/his students with the role of expertise. (Even very young children will instinctively recognise that this role is being assumed and will probably feel some excitement at being drawn into the play.) Second, the students are given a structure with which to review, synthesise and sequence the key points of the story, one that allows everyone in a large class to take a role. *Agency*, *role* and *deconstructive strategies* are being employed, and a range of interpretive functions of literacy are being addressed.

The teacher can then move into the frame partially described at the beginning of this chapter. "How would the Bears feel when they come home?" the teacher might prompt. "How would you feel if you came back and found your house trashed? What would you do?" The suggestion to call the police might come from a student or from the teacher. The teacher then passes a phone (imagined) to one the students: "Here, you make the call. I'll be the police at the other end."

The teacher in role as a policewoman provokes the member of the Bear family to be explicit about what has happened. "You'll have to put it in writing," she says. "Can you write us a letter?" In shadow role the teacher and the students write the Bears' letter to the police. *Agency, role* and *deconstruction* are again important. *Framing* also plays a vital role. In a real-life setting, dealing with the police is an arena children would leave to an adult. But while they are in collective role as the Bears they can allow themselves the freedom to interpret, make decisions and shape the efficacy of their communication.

In the next frame the police come for Goldilocks. First the teacher helps the students pick a Goldilocks, who will initially hide at the back of the room. The rest of the group becomes Goldilocks's family. The drama begins with the teacher in role as a police officer coming to Goldilocks's house to arrest her. The Bears' letter could be projected on to a screen and the family asked to read it.

The teacher plays the role in a way that provokes the family to plead Goldilocks's case rather than give her up, but the officer is not easily persuaded. After all, the Bears' complaint is substantial and their family were genuinely aggrieved. The onus is on Goldilocks's family to make reasonable suggestions. *Framing* is being manipulated here to provoke the students as audience/actors to explore both sides of the conflict, and once again it allows children to explore values and decision making they might in real life see as being owned by their elders.

When the police officer is happy with the suggestions made by the family, she or he leaves. It is now over to the family to coach Goldilocks on what she has to do to sort things out with the Bears. A contract might be written out. In this frame the teacher might side-coach, prompting the family if they need it. The level and complexity of ethical thinking that very young students demonstrate in this work is often amazing. The *framing* gives them permission to experiment, and *role* allows them to engage both emotionally and intellectually.

The drama could be continued to encompass whatever specific literacy (or other) skills the teacher wishes to develop or review. For example, there might be further negotiation with the Bears before reconciliation is achieved; or there might be a formal letter of apology or further reports to the police. A celebratory finish might include a class-composed song or poem about saying sorry. There might be a magazine report about the incident and its resolution, or the taping of interviews for a television documentary.

As well as being a strong motivator, drama is a powerful reinforcer. As students perform tasks within role, they re-form their capacity to do similar tasks in real life. As they take the mantle of expertise in drama, they begin to preview and celebrate the results of the learning they are engaged in.

Mallory House

Whereas the Goldilocks drama was designed for junior classes, *Mallory House* is intended for slightly older students—intermediate or junior secondary. The concept for the drama has been adapted from O'Neill's drama *The Haunted House* (O'Neill & Lambert, 1982). Potentially this can be an extended and rich drama, so here I will focus on some of the key scenes that might be used to promote literacy.

The drama opens with a notice (on the classroom board) of an advertisement in the local newspaper: "$500 to those willing to spend a night at Mallory House. Those interested please come to …" The classroom is given as the venue and the teacher briefly explains that the students will take the roles of people who have come in response to the advertisement. The drama begins as she (for narrative ease we will assume a female teacher here) steps into role and, glancing speculatively around the room, remarks, "I am so glad to see so many of you here. Let me introduce myself: I am Mrs Carson, and it is I who placed that advertisement in the paper. I've called this meeting to answer any questions you may have. I take it you all have heard of Mallory House?"

In the discussion that ensues she reveals that Mallory House is a 150-year-old property, some kilometres out of town, and that it was once one of the stately houses of the district but it has fallen into disrepair. She is a little cagey, giving a minimum of information while pretending to welcome questions, but she does let it emerge that those who wish to earn the money will be taken by bus to the house and will be paid if they are still there the following morning; that there is no electricity or running water in the house, but food will be provided; and that the house is most definitely not haunted.

In this first frame it is only the teacher who steps fully into role. The class assumes a shadow group role, whereby they develop suspicions about the house in the fictional frame. The interaction within the drama frame prompts students to examine the difference between text and subtext—between what is overtly said and what is implied by the evasions of the plausible Mrs Carson. If appropriate, the teacher might lead the discussion to consideration of subtext, evasion or the kind of questioning strategies the participants used. Alternatively, she might lead it to a discussion of body language, or emotional responses. At this stage the students are exercising little control over the drama and so their agency resides principally in the ways they critically reflect on the character's motivation and the house's history in the fictional frame.

In a cross-curricular context, it might be useful to elicit students' speculations about the house through a stylised movement sequence depicting dreams. The next literacy task, however, sends the class looking for further information about Mallory House. This part of the work could go in a number of directions. The teacher could, in advance, organise some books about the period and the region, and maybe create some newspaper articles or letters for the participants to discover. Or she could lead them to Miss Lawrence.

Miss Lawrence, the teacher explains, is an old lady who has lived all her life in a small house just a kilometre or so from Mallory House, and the teacher sets up the students in groups to plan the questions they would like to ask her. Planning questions is a language curriculum skill and a research skill, and the teacher might want to discuss the kind of questions that lead to rich answers and the kinds that shut off discussion. There might also be some discussion about how to approach an old lady.

Each group selects one of their number to interview Miss Lawrence. The others sit around the room as "flies on the wall". If they feel they can move the story forward, they tag one of the interviewers and take their place, sustaining the role. The teacher takes the role of Miss Lawrence, who is sweet, welcoming, but obviously unwilling to revisit painful memories. She does, however, reveal that when she was still a young girl "a great injustice" took place in the house. At this stage, although the students are moving further into role, their characterisation is less important than their task. However, their agency is growing. In the next stages they will be allowed to use their deductive imagination, and previous research, to shape the story.

So what, the teacher, out of role asks, was the great injustice? The students' task in groups is to construct, perhaps in freeze frame, the climactic moment of the great injustice. The value of freeze frames is that they require clear definition of characterisation, relationship, action and reaction. However, minimalistic dialogue and movement can also be used to animate the freeze frame.

The history of the house and its inhabitants might be explored through further dramatic action, but might also be explored through other text forms that suit the goals of the literacy programme, such as writing the diary of one of the characters, creating an account of the events in a faded newspaper of the period or creating a video documentary. The drama might also explore, through a range of text forms, the subsequent history of the house. For example, what was the gossip from the wider community when the house was later put up for auction? What happened when a new family moved in? What if a ghost of a character from one of the earlier scenes joined them at dinner? Or a current events documentary might research Mrs Carson's career and her connection to the story. The specific literacy tasks depend on the pedagogical aims of the teacher.

Implications for practice

The use of role and fictional frame allow students to have agency and to engage creatively and emotionally as well as conceptually with their learning. They also offer a palette of deconstructive strategies. In this way, the use of drama serves not only to motivate students to read and write, but also provides a direct teaching tool for a range of ways to produce and interpret text. As students play with the possibilities offered by the fictional frame, they can engage in the development of real skills. However, note that although any kind of drama might be fun and build participants' confidence and self-esteem, the teacher needs to strategically manipulate contexts, roles, target activities and tensions in order to provoke specific learning. The dramas offered in the above discussion might provide part of a pool for teachers to draw on, extend and adapt.

References

Carr, M., & Claxton, G. (2004). Tracking the development of learning disposition. In H. Daniels & A. Edwards (Eds.), *RoutledgeFalmer reader in psychology of education* (pp. 106–132). London: RoutledgeFalmer.

DeZutter, S. (2007). Play as group improvement. In O. Saracho & B. Spodek (Eds.), *Contemporary perspectives on social learning in early childhood education* (pp. 217–242). Charlotte, NC: Information Age.

Ehri, L. C. (2006). More about phonics: Findings and reflections. In K. A. Dougherty Stahl & M. C. McKenna (Eds.), *Reading research at work: Foundations of effective practice* (pp. 155–169). New York: Guilford Press.

Gardner, H. (1993). *Frames of mind: The theory of multiple intelligences.* London: Fontana.

Gee, J. P. (2000). *An introduction to discourse analysis: Theory and method.* London: Routledge.

Greenwood, J. (2005). *Playing with curriculum: Drama for junior classes.* Invercargill: Essential resources [2nd edition of *I Can Feed the Reindeer*].

Greenwood, J., & Sæbo, A. (2009, September). *Bringing the textbook to life: Using creative group processes in the classroom.* Paper presented at European Conference on Educational Research, Vienna.

Healy, A. (2008). *Multiliteracies and diversity in education: New pedagogies for expanding landscapes.* South Melbourne and Oxford: Oxford University Press.

Heathcote, D., & Bolton, G. (1995). *Drama for learning: Dorothy Heathcote's mantle of the expert approach to education.* Portsmouth, NH: Heinemann.

Millar, C., & Saxton, J. (2004). *Into the story: Language in action through drama.* Portsmouth, NH: Heinemann.

O'Neill, C., & Lambert, A. (1982). *Drama structures.* Portsmouth, NH: Heinemann.

O'Toole, P., & Dunn, J. (2002). *Pretending to learn.* Brisbane: Longman.

Pressley, M. (2006). *Reading instruction that works: The case for balanced teaching*. New York: Guilford Press.

Schunk, D., Pintrich, P., & Meece, J. (2008). *Motivation in education: Theory, research and applications* (3rd ed.). Upper Saddle River, NJ: Pearson.

Wagner, B. J. (1998). *Educational drama and language arts: What research shows*. Portsmouth, NH : Heinemann.

CHAPTER 12
Multiliteracies and learning in a new age

Nicola Yelland

Introduction

Becoming literate (and numerate) is regarded as a fundamental component of, and a success indicator for, the economic prosperity of a nation. Thus, the goal of achieving high literacy rates is viewed as an imperative for the education of citizens, and consequently much time, effort and funds are poured into creating what are considered to be effective literacy policies and practices in schools. Further, much is made of literacy outcomes using comparisons of various countries' achievements in education. All these imperatives combine to create a context for a simplistic view of literacy that can be quantified and measured, so that policy makers and politicians are able to show that the system they oversee is supporting increased levels of literacy in the population.

A visit to the websites of various education departments across the world indicates that the fundamental components of literacy are regularly viewed as consisting of reading, writing, spelling, viewing, talking and listening. Recently there has been much emphasis in English-speaking countries on the importance of teaching phonics. Those who support this stance say that they want to ensure that students in schools are able to have the strategies to decode words, and they view the teaching of phonics as essential to this process. Other educationalists stress the importance of contexts for becoming literate, and while recognising that the skills inherent in knowing sounds are useful they view it as one technique among many and stress that the ability to create, view, interpret and create multimodal texts and interpret content critically is an essential aspect of literacy for the 21st century. In this way we have experienced what have been called the "literacy wars" (see, for example, "Casualties of the literacy wars", 2008), where those who tout a traditional view of literacy in terms of the ability to read and write are pitched against those with a broader and more contemporary view that incorporates digital literacies and an ability to critically interpret a range and variety of modern-day texts and images.

So, while all educators accept the importance of being literate in the 21st century, how do we reconcile these views into a coherent conceptualisation of literacy and then determine what forms literacy teaching should take in schools today? Millennial kids live very different lives from those of previous generations (Yelland, 2007). They are highly motivated to create and share diverse multimodal texts in new and dynamic ways. The most recent survey of media use by US children (Kaiser Family Foundation, 2009) found that "The amount of time young people spend with media has grown to where it's even more than a full-time work week" (p. 1). I recognise that in order to do this we need to be able to have some basic skills that enable us to decode and create multimodal texts of our own, and this includes the teaching of phonics as a skill in English-speaking countries. However, my view of the teaching of phonics would probably differ considerably from that of a more conservative teacher, who might require children in their first year of formal schooling to be restricted to one sound a week, and who might drill and teach them with out-of-context worksheets and mundane activities that require them to find and circle sounds and colour in pictures of objects.

In this chapter I discuss the notion of being multiliterate in the 21st century. I argue that we need to broaden our conceptualisation of literacy to incorporate fluency with digital technologies, which requires a consideration of the various modalities of learning. New technologies motivate students to engage in literate practices in dynamic ways in the 21st century. The concept of multiliteracies (New London Group, 1996) enables us to think about contexts, modalities and ways of knowing that incorporate new technologies in this new era. Here I will interrogate what this entails for teachers and learners in today's schools and provide examples of learning scenarios from empirical research studies. I contend that if we fail to address and include new technologies and a multiliteracies perspective, schools risk becoming an anachronism.

New literacies and multiliteracies

Luke (2006) has a view of literacy as the acquisition of a "malleable repertoire of practices", not a set of specific (literacy) skills. He contends:

> Learning to be literate is like learning to be an artisan in a guild, to play an instrument in an ensemble, like acquiring a craft within a community whose art and forms of life are dynamic, rather than a robotic acquisition and automization of core skills. (p. xi)

As previously stated, literacy in schools traditionally emphasises reading, writing, spelling, listening and speaking with paper-based printed texts. However, it is readily apparent that new technologies have enabled links to be made between the whole range of visual, aural, spatial and gestural modes of communication (New London Group, 1996). These are the new texts that 21st century students are fluent with and interact with on a daily basis in their lives outside of school. Yelland, Hill, and Mulhearn (2004) have noted the importance of this multimodal context of multiliteracies for emergent literacy learners, which is an integral part of their lives before coming to formal schooling. Moll and his colleagues (1992) have argued that children bring "funds of knowledge" to school from their homes and communities, and that we should be building on them in early childhood settings in order to connect with children's life worlds. These funds of knowledge are multimodal in nature, and with the increasing use of media in the home children have ready access to them on a very frequent basis (Yelland et al., 2004). Linking them to school practices will not only enable students to make the connections necessary for deep learning, but also represents contexts in which they are highly motivated to learn.

Lankshear and Knobel (2004) argue for new mind sets to address the interfaces that occur between literacy, technology and social practices and suggest that a variety of new literacies need to be recognised since there are many ways to represent ideas and communicate with others. Kress (2003) has suggested, in fact, that representation and meaning making undergo significant changes in logic and organisation as we move from a linguistic print environment to contexts of multimodal communication and information exchange. He argues, for example, that speech and language are governed by the logics of time and chronological sequence. Images, in contrast, are governed by a logic of space and function, where meaning can be constructed from placement, size, colour and shape. This means that messages can be conveyed in completely different ways, and that this will influence how the final "product" is viewed and interpreted (see also Lankshear & Knobel, 2004).

The work of Leu (2000, 2002) has revealed that traditional conceptualisations of literacy that are confined to print media significantly undermine children's ability to succeed at school. His work has explored the ways in which the Internet has enabled children to experience new opportunities for reading and writing that bring with them new forms of social and cultural interactions that were not possible in previous times.

In thinking about becoming literate in a digital world, Marsh (2004) has noted that we should be aware of the techno-literacy practices that children are engaged with and fluent in prior to their entering school, since they are an integral part of their emergent literacy skills that should be built on in literacy sessions in schools. She found that when the literacy practices children use at home and in their local community are examined, they reveal a complex range of contemporary literacy skills, knowledge and understanding that are used on a regular and frequent basis for authentic purposes. As a result, Marsh actively challenges the use of the phrases "pre-readers" and "pre-writers", and suggests that all the communicative competencies that children demonstrate in their preschool years need to be acknowledged and used in school contexts.

Multimodality

Contemporary conceptualisations of literacy recognise the multiple modalities that we use to communicate ideas and meanings. These include the linguistic, visual, aural, gestural and spatial. The lives of contemporary children are saturated with multimodal information that influences and shapes their linguistic competence (Pahl & Rowsell, 2006). This involves them in becoming skilled at:
- taking in information from the environment
- manipulating symbols and systems
- playing and making sense of the world
- developing a sense of self and communicative norms.

Jewitt (2006) has said that "all texts are multimodal and modes are always interconnected in a text" (p. 40). In traditional printed texts, for example, the meaning and message conveyed by the printed word are affected by colour, size, font and placement. Children should have the opportunity to explore the variations in conventions and designs of each mode, then consider the impact these have in relation to one another. In this way they will become fluent at being able to accurately read or make meaning from multimodal texts. Each mode has a system of conventions and resources that affects the ways in which meaning making and communication are enabled, and as students "take up these resources, transform them and design meaning with them" (Jewitt, 2006, p. 40), they advance down a pathway to becoming multiliterate.

What does "becoming multiliterate" mean? The New London Group (1996) used the term "multiliteracies" to link print, visual and audio texts, which they said were becoming increasingly prevalent in our lives. The term is also related to the communicative skills of speaking, writing and reading (Hagood, 2000). The raison d'être for a new term was based on the premise that making meaning from texts was become increasingly complex as a result of major changes in our social world in the latter part of the 20th century. They used two instances to support this view. First, the way in which the mass media permeate everything we see and do is essentially carried out in linguistic and visual modes. This means that we need to be able to read them effectively and derive our own meanings about their effectiveness and purpose. Second, everyday actions require that we co-ordinate and make sense of linguistic meaning in written texts, together with other modalities such as the spatial. In this way, a visit to a shopping mall requires that we be able to negotiate signs that are both written and use visual symbols, as well as to understand the spatial architecture of the building. They stipulated that "All meaning making is multimodal. All written text is also visually designed" (p. 81), and that spoken language is "a matter of audio design as much as it is a matter of linguistic design understood as grammatical relationships" (p. 81).

Their work suggests there are three main aspects to becoming multiliterate that we should consider:

- multimodality: being able to read the layers of meaning in multimodal forms of communication and "texts", which include linguistic, visual, aural, spatial and gestural modes
- social and cultural practices in contemporary times: developing a sense of self and a repertoire of capabilities and understanding that enable meaning making and participation in contemporary social and cultural practices
- acquiring knowledge for contemporary living: learning to learn, be, live and know in order to lead personally fulfilling lives, contribute to family life and engage in local and global communities.

As previously noted, being fluent in multimodal formats enables new forms of communication and meaning making. Engaging in social and cultural practices requires that we link existing knowledge to new experiences and make new connections and contextual associations as a result of this. It requires reflection and critical analysis so that we are able to decide on the best way to communicate ideas or make sense of our experiences. This requires a rethinking of what is involved in being literate, because it goes beyond a skills-based approach.

Multiliteracies in action

In what follows I present three examples of children's work that engaged them in representing their ideas with different modalities in multiliteracies projects. The first two simply focus on the *media* with which it is possible to combine visual, aural and linguistic components. The third example describes a curriculum context in which an investigation took place. The topic spanned the traditional curriculum areas found in Australian primary schools and occurred in a context in which the teacher wanted to support children's investigative learning using a variety of modalities and information sources. I suggest that all three represent contexts in which the students are highly motivated to learn and communicate what they have learnt in multimodal formats.

It seems as if the advent of the iPod fundamentally changed how we interact with aural and visual modes since it became commercially available. Podcasts enable learners to combine sounds, texts and visual representations as a communication medium. In the example provided here, two Year 1 (six years of age) children created pictures with *Kid Pix* to illustrate the various activities they enjoyed, one of which was swimming (see Figures 1 to 3). They itemised the equipment they used for swimming, created a narrative around the swimming events they had participated in and stated why they enjoyed them so much. They were able to record their voices accompanying the text, and the final product of their work could be viewed in printed form as well as on an MP3 player. The teachers had to "teach" this new form of literacy to the children before they were able to use it for their own purposes, but they readily appropriated it and extended its use with both digital and video clips and graphics. Some of the children even created their own music with *Garage Band* to accompany their visual creations.

In another example (Figure 4), a teacher enabled new immigrants to think about contrasts and similarities between their old and new environments in a PowerPoint presentation, which was accompanied by a sound recording of their voices speaking the words. The PowerPoint could be viewed digitally or in a hard copy of the book, which was laminated so it could be taken home and also kept in the library corner of the classroom.

Finally, in the topic on endangered species, a Year 3 (eight years of age) class selected and researched a particular animal in small groups and discussed where the animal can be currently found in the world, its salient features and why it is under threat, and described its habitat and source of food. The project was designed by the teacher so that her students could experience how to find

Figure 1 Swimming equipment

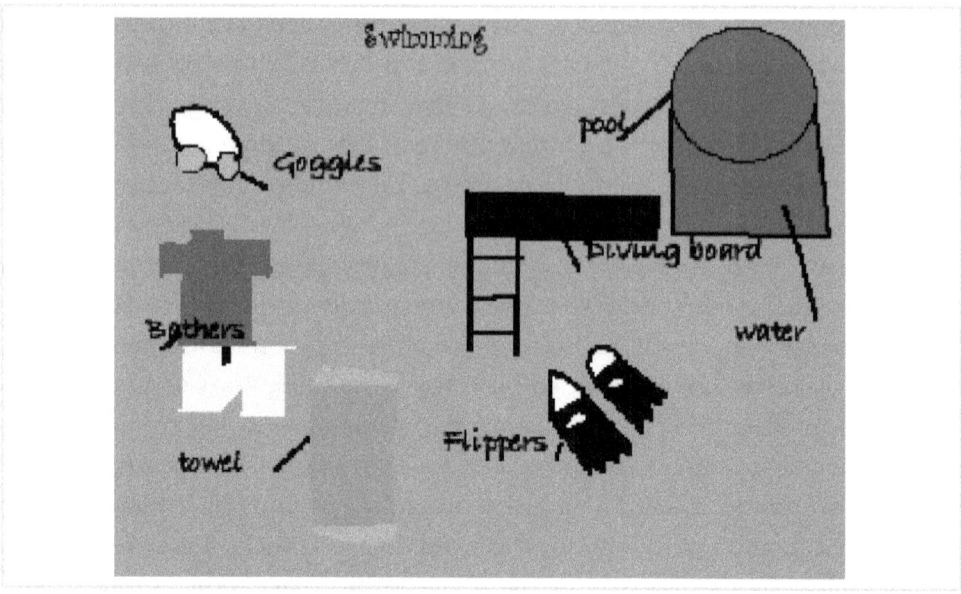

Figure 2 Jack likes swimming

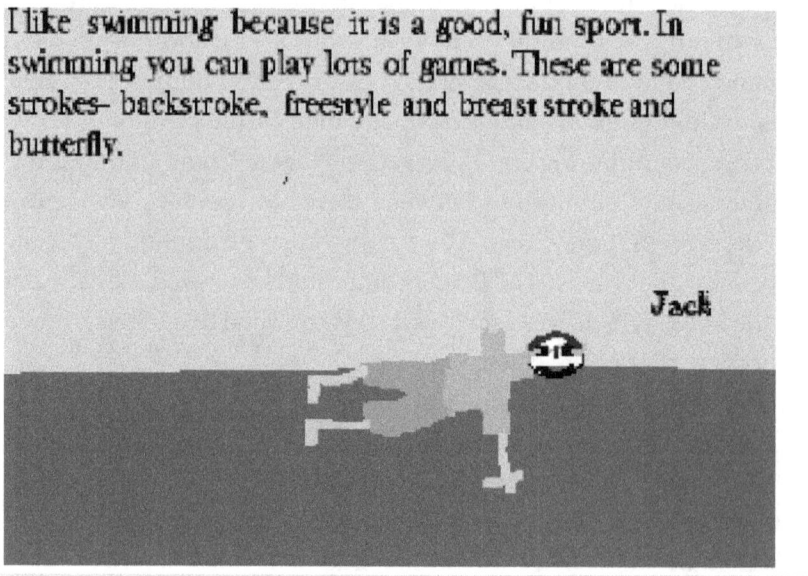

Figure 3 Payton on swimming is fun

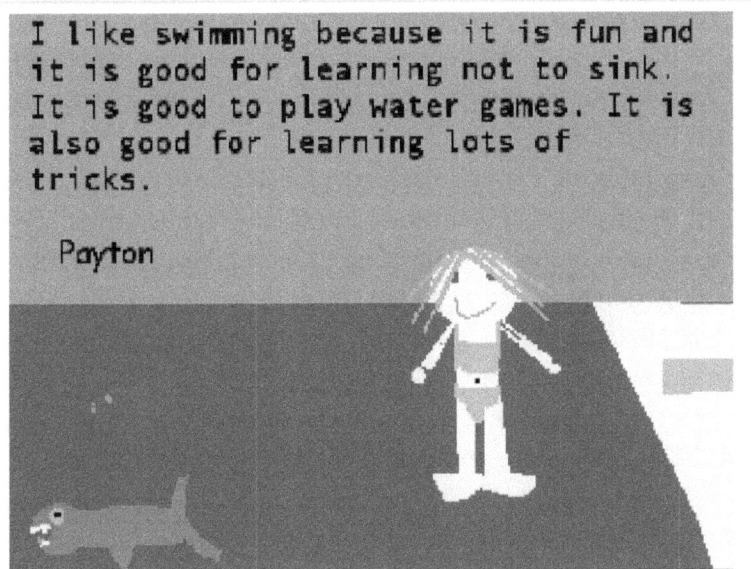

Figure 4 When we came to school in Australia

information from a variety of sources. They were encouraged to use multiple formats to present the information they had acquired. Information was sourced from a visit to the city zoo, seeking out expert opinion from people who worked in the area, books from the library and various sites on the Internet, which were both text- and visual/video-based.

In this investigation the students had a particular framework to work within, but they were not constrained by it and many of them extended their investigations to look at possible solutions to the problem of species becoming extinct. This was the first investigation of this type by the class of eight-year-olds and the teacher had to provide scaffolding to support their work while giving them choices about which particular direction their work might go. The teacher had specific goals in terms of learning outcomes for literacy as well as for her science and social studies curriculum, and she linked these effectively in an integrated approach in a topic of interest to the children in her class. Once the children had collected and assembled their information, they presented it to their class and created a Web-based portal to show their collective work to their parents and to other members of the school community who had access to the school's website.

Figure 5 illustrates one such investigation into the plight of the snow leopard. It shows the flow diagram the teacher created with the children to conceptualise the project as a whole, as well as her goals for the resource-based learning project. The rest of the figure contains a *Kid Pix* drawing of a scientific diagram of the snow leopard, a digital photo of the snow leopard and a second *Kid Pix* depiction of the animal's habitat. Finally, the front of the shared Web page is shown to illustrate the range of endangered species that were studied by the class.

This multiliteracies project, like the previous examples, consisted of projects that were varied and interesting. They were the result of investigations that were thorough and demanding in terms of finding information and transforming it into a narrative that was meaningful and conveyed new understanding to an audience. At the end of the project the children said that not only had they enjoyed the work but also that they had learnt a lot about endangered species. They also discussed the techniques and strategies they deployed in order to create their final presentations and articulated the ways in which they had contributed to their

Figure 5 Endangered species—the snow leopard

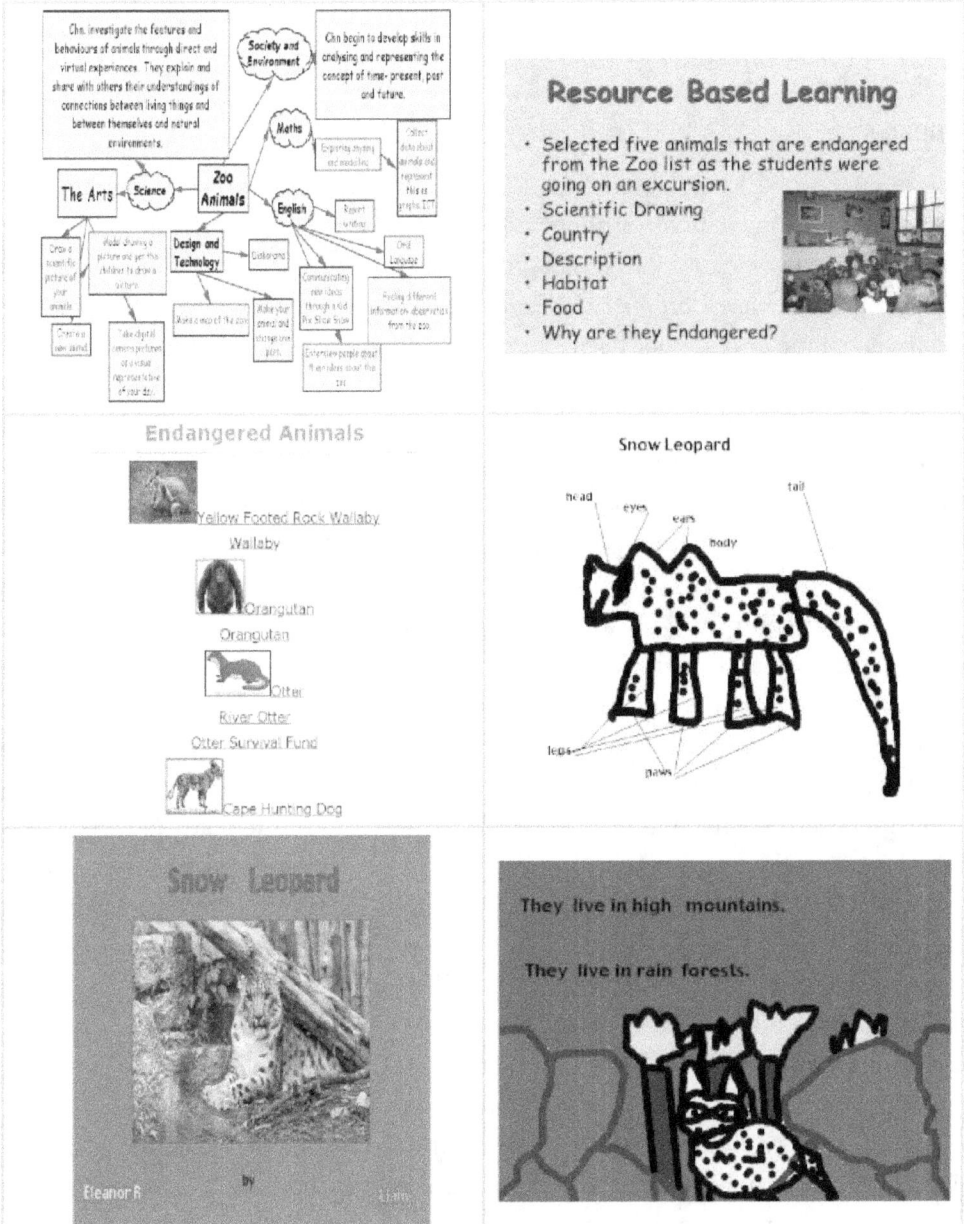

knowledge building about endangered species. This learning was multimodal and embedded as social practice within the context of the classroom, school and community they lived in.

Summary

Luke (2006, p. xii) has stated that schools and education systems remain in a transition state and are struggling to keep up with the rapid changes in society and technology. He maintains that schools are still encouraging "mono-cultural, print children" based on curriculum practices that are designed to "reproduce relatively static and stable disciplinary knowledge". This cultivates "local and often narrowly parochial identities and national ideologies".

New technologies and the social practices that facilitate them require us to reconsider what we mean when we talk about the foundational knowledge, skills and conventions of practice and the underlying systems and structures of the various modes of literate practices. This means broadening what is valued as literacy to encompass the various modes, and also attending more closely to providing children with a balance of foundational, relational, critical and creative literacy and learning opportunities. In this way, children will have the opportunity to learn about relevant traditions, make links and connections to their own experiences and cultural heritage and be encouraged to express and develop their ideas in relation to new possibilities.

In this chapter I have attempted to show that a multiliteracies perspective is highly motivating, and relevant and valuable for contemporary times, since it incorporates the broad-based social and cultural communicative practices that determine what constitutes literacy in the 21st century. Systems and school practices still promote print literacy to the forefront of literacy without considering the ways in which it can be used effectively in a variety of discourses. Locating literacy as a social and cultural practice helps us to understand how particular ways of knowing and communicating can marginalise some children and privilege others.

The pedagogy of multiliteracies (New London Group, 1996) enables a view of literacy that considers multimodal communication, and new technologies have created alternative "reading paths" and texts that can be considered as "traces of people, contexts and implied practices" (Pahl & Rowsell, p. 38). In this way, becoming literate implies a level of consciousness (Freire, 1973; Searle, 1993) and the capacity to live dignified, aware, reflective and fulfilling lives.

References

Casualties of the literacy wars. (2008, 19 January). *Sydney Morning Herald*. Retrieved from http://www.smh.com.au/articles/2008/01/18/1200620211552.html

Freire, P. (1973). *Education for critical consciousness*. New York: Seabury Press.

Hagood, M. C. (2000). New times, new millennium, new literacies. *Reading Research and Instruction, 39*(4), 311–328.

Jewitt, C. (2006). *Technology, literacy and learning: A multimodal approach*. Abingdon, England: Routledge.

Kaiser Family Foundation. (2009). *Generation M2: Media in the lives of 8 to 18 year olds*. [Press release.] Available at http://www.kff.org/entmedia/entmedia012010nr.cfm

Kress, G. (2003). *Literacy in the new media*. London: Routledge.

Lankshear, C., & Knobel, M. (2004). *New literacies: Changing knowledge and classroom learning*. Buckingham: Open University Press.

Leu, D. (2000). Our children's future: Changing the focus of literacy and literacy instruction. *Reading Teacher, 53*, 424–431.

Leu, D. (2002). The new literacies: Research on reading instruction with the Internet and other digital technologies. In A. E. Farstrup & S. J. Samuels (Eds.), *What research has to say about reading instruction* (3rd ed., pp. 310–337). Newark, DE: International Reading Association.

Luke, A. (2006). Foreword. In K. Pahl & J. Roswell (Eds.), *Literacy and education: Understanding the new literacy studies in the classroom* (pp. x–xiv). London: Paul Chapman.

Marsh, J. A. (2004). *BBC child of our time: Young children's use of popular culture, media and new technologies*. Sheffield: University of Sheffield.

Moll, L. C., Amanti, C., Neff, D. & Gonzales, N. (1992). Funds of knowledge for teaching: Using a qualitative approach to connect homes and classrooms. *Theory into Practice, 31*(2), 132–141.

New London Group. (1996). A pedagogy of multiliteracies. *Harvard Educational Review, 60*(1), 66–92.

Pahl, K., & Rowsell, J. (2006). *Travel notes from the new literacy studies: Instances of practice*. Clevedon: Multilingual Matters.

Searle, J. R. (1993). The problem of consciousness. *Consciousness & Cognition, 2*, 310–319.

Yelland, N. J. (2007). *Shift to the future: Rethinking learning with new technologies in education.* New York: Routledge.

Yelland, N. J., Hill, S., & Mulhearn, G. (2004). Using information and communication technologies for playing and learning in the information age. *International Journal of Learning, 11*, 1603–1618.

Authors

Jo Fletcher is a senior lecturer in Literacy Education at the College of Education, University of Canterbury, New Zealand.
Email: jo.fletcher@canterbury.ac.nz

Faye Parkhill is a senior lecturer in Literacy Education at the College of Education, University of Canterbury, New Zealand.
Email: faye.parkhill@canterbury.ac.nz

Gail Gillon is Pro-Vice-Chancellor, at the College of Education, University of Canterbury, New Zealand.
Email: gail.gillon@canterbury.ac.nz

Teresa Cremin is a professor in the Faculty of Education and Language Studies at the The Open University, United Kingdom.
Email: t.m.cremin@open.ac.uk

Noella Mackenzie is a lecturer in Literacy at the Murray School of Education, Charles Sturt University, Australia.
Email: nmackenzie@csu.edu.au

Judy M. Parr is a professor in the Faculty of Education, The University of Auckland, New Zealand.
Email: jm.parr@auckland.ac.nz

Dr Kathryn Glasswell is a senior lecturer in the School of Education and Professional Studies, Griffith University, Gold Coast, Australia.
Email: k.glasswell@griffith.edu.au

Elspeth McCartney is a reader in the Division of Speech and Language Therapy, University of Strathclyde, Scotland.
Email: e.mccartney@strath.ac.uk

Sue Ellis is a reader in the Literacy and Language in the Department of Childhood and Primary Studies, University of Strathclyde, Scotland.
Email: sue.ellis@strath.ac.uk

Brigid McNeill is a lecturer in Language and Literacy Development in the College of Education, University of Canterbury, New Zealand.
Email: brigid.mcneill@canterbury.ac.nz

John Everatt is a professor in Reading Development and Disorders in the College of Education, University of Canterbury, New Zealand.
Email: john.everatt@canterbury.ac.nz

Gavin Reid is a consultant in the Centre for Child Evaluation and Teaching, Kuwait.
Email: gavinreid66@googlemail.com

Marleen F. Westerveld is a senior research fellow in Child Language Development in the College of Education, University of Canterbury, New Zealand
Email: marleen.westerveld@canterbury.ac.nz

Angus Hikairo Macfarlane is Professor of Maori Research at the University of Canterbury, New Zealand.
Email: angus.macfarlane@canterbury.ac.nz

Amosa Fa'afoi is a lecturer in Maori, Social and Cultural Studies in Education at the University of Canterbury, New Zealand.
Email: amosa.faafoi@canterbury.ac.nz

Leali'ie'e Tufulasi Taleni is a Pacific Education Adviser at the University of Canterbury, New Zealand.
Email: tufulasi.taleni@canterbury.ac.nz

Janinka Greenwood is a professor in Drama Education in the College of Education, University of Canterbury, New Zealand.
Email: janinka.greenwood@canterbury.ac.nz

Nicola Yelland is a professor in the Hong Kong Institute of Education, Hong Kong.
Email: yelland@ied.edu.hk

www.ingramcontent.com/pod-product-compliance
Lightning Source LLC
Chambersburg PA
CBHW081332230426
43667CB00018B/2904